Common CORE **Writing to** ...

Table of Contents

Introduction

What Is the Common Core?

The Common Core State Standards are an initiative by states to set shared, consistent, and clear criteria for what students are expected to learn. This helps teachers and parents know what they need to do to help students. The standards are designed to be rigorous and pertinent to the real world. They reflect the knowledge and skills that young people need for success in college and careers.

If your state has joined the Common Core State Standards Initiative, then teachers are required to incorporate these standards into their lesson plans. Students need targeted practice in order to meet grade-level standards and expectations, and thereby be promoted to the next grade.

What Does It Mean to Write to Texts?

One of the most important instructional shifts in the Common Core State Standards is writing to texts, or sources. What exactly does this mean? Haven't standardized assessments always used reading texts as a springboard to writing? Yes, but the required writing hasn't always been DEPENDENT on the key ideas and details in a text.

A prompt that is non-text-dependent asks students to rely on prior knowledge or experience. In fact, students could likely carry out the writing without reading the text at all. The writing does not need to include ideas, information, and key vocabulary from the text.

Writing to texts requires students to analyze, clarify, and cite information they read in the text. The writing reveals whether students have performed a close reading, because it is designed to elicit ideas, information, and key vocabulary from the text as well as students' own evidence-based inferences and conclusions. These are all skills that prepare them for the grades ahead, college, the workplace, and real-world applications in their adult daily lives.

An example of a passage with non-text-dependent and text-dependent sample prompts is provided on page 3.

Simple and Compound Machines

1. A simple machine is a tool that does work with one movement. Like all machines, a simple machine makes work easier. It has few or no moving parts and uses energy to do work. A lever, a wedge, a screw, a pulley, a wheel and axle, and an inclined plane are all simple machines.

2. You use simple machines all the time, too. If you have ever played on a seesaw or walked up a ramp, then you have used a simple machine. If you have opened a door, eaten with a spoon, cut with scissors, or zipped up a zipper, you have used a simple machine.

3. A compound machine is made of two or more simple machines. For example, the pedals, wheels, and gears on a bicycle are wheels and axles, and the hand brakes on the handlebars are levers. Cars, airplanes, watches, and washing machines are also compound machines. Compound machines can do the work of many simple machines at the same time.

4. Life would be very different if we did not have machines. Work would be much harder, and playing wouldn't be as much fun.

Standard	Sample Prompt: Non-Text-Dependent	Sample Prompt: Text-Dependent
W.3.1 (Opinion/ Argument)	Do you prefer zippers, buttons, buckles, or another type of fastener for your clothing? Why?	The author makes three claims in the last paragraph. Choose one of the claims, tell whether you agree or disagree, and support your opinion with evidence from the text.
W.3.2 (Informative/ Explanatory)	Think about a machine you have used to do a task. How did you use it? How did using the machine make the task easier?	Compare and contrast simple and compound machines. Use details from the text to support your explanation.
W.3.3 (Narrative)	Write a story in which a character invents a machine that no one has seen or heard of before.	Imagine that all the machines mentioned in the passage disappeared for twenty-four hours. Write a journal entry about how your life was different that day and what you learned.

Using This Book

How Does This Book Help Students?

This book is organized into four main sections: Writing Mini-Lessons, Practice Texts with Prompts, Graphic Organizers and Checklists, and Rubrics and Assessments. All mini-lessons and practice pages are self-contained and may be used in any order that meets the needs of students. The elements of this book work together to provide students with the tools they need to be able to master the range of skills and application as required by the Common Core.

1. Mini-Lessons for Opinion/Argument, Informative/Explanatory, and Narrative Writing

Writing mini-lessons prepare students to use writing as a way to state and support opinions, demonstrate understanding of the subjects they are studying, and convey real and imagined experiences. The mini-lessons are organized in the order of the standards, but you may wish to do them with your class in an order that matches your curriculum. For each type of writing the first mini-lesson covers responding to one text, while the second mini-lesson models how to respond to multiple texts.

Each mini-lesson begins with a lesson plan that provides step-by-step instruction.

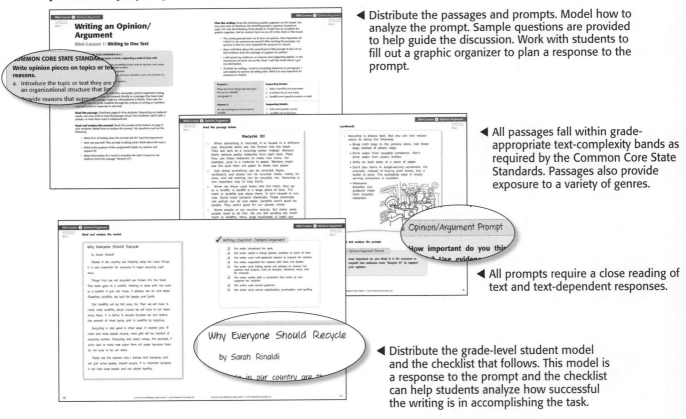

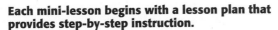

◄ Distribute the passages and prompts. Model how to analyze the prompt. Sample questions are provided to help guide the discussion. Work with students to fill out a graphic organizer to plan a response to the prompt.

◄ All passages fall within grade-appropriate text-complexity bands as required by the Common Core State Standards. Passages also provide exposure to a variety of genres.

◄ All prompts require a close reading of text and text-dependent responses.

◄ Distribute the grade-level student model and the checklist that follows. This model is a response to the prompt and the checklist can help students analyze how successful the writing is in accomplishing the task.

2. Practice Texts with Prompts

Passages and prompts provide students with real experience writing to a single text and multiple texts. The first ten lessons require students to respond to one text. The last ten require students to respond to multiple texts.

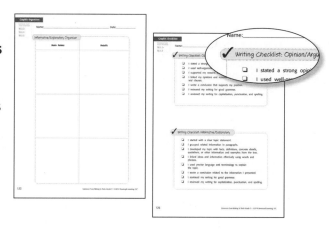

Each passage or pair of passages is followed by three text-dependent prompts: Opinion/Argument, Informative/Explanatory, and Narrative. You may wish to assign a particular prompt, have students choose one, or have them execute each type of writing over a longer period of time.

For more information on how to use this section, see page 48.

3. Graphic Organizers and Checklists

For each type of writing, you can distribute a corresponding graphic organizer and checklist to help students plan and evaluate their writing.

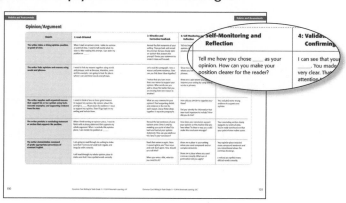

4. Rubrics and Assessments

The section includes Evaluation Rubrics to guide your assessment and scoring of students' responses. Based on your observations of students' writing, use the differentiated rubrics. These are designed to help you conduct meaningful conferences with students and will help differentiate your interactions to match students' needs.

For each score a student receives in the Evaluation Rubrics, responsive prompts are provided. These gradual-release prompts scaffold writers toward mastery of each writing type.

COMMON CORE
STATE STANDARD
W.3.1

Writing an Opinion/ Argument

Mini-Lesson 1: **Writing to One Text**

> **COMMON CORE STATE STANDARD W.3.1**
>
> **Write opinion pieces on topics or texts, supporting a point of view with reasons.**
>
> a. Introduce the topic or text they are writing about, state an opinion, and create an organizational structure that lists reasons.
>
> b. Provide reasons that support the opinion.
>
> c. Use linking words and phrases (e.g., *because, therefore, since, for example*) to connect opinion and reasons.
>
> d. Provide a concluding statement or section.

Explain to students that they will often encounter opinion/argument writing prompts that instruct them to respond directly to a passage they have read. Tell them that the passage might be informational or fiction. Then take the following steps to guide students through the process of writing an opinion/ argument piece in response to one text.

Read the passage. Distribute pages 8–9 to students. Depending on students' needs, you may wish to read the passage aloud, have students read it with a partner, or have them read it independently.

Read and analyze the prompt. Read the prompt at the bottom of page 9 with students. Model how to analyze the prompt. Ask questions such as the following:

- *What form of writing does the prompt ask for?* (opinion/argument)
- *How can you tell?* (The prompt is asking what I think about the topic.)
- *What is the purpose of the assignment?* (state my opinion and support it)
- *What information do I need to complete the task?* (I need to use evidence from the passage "Recycle It!")

COMMON CORE
STATE STANDARD
W.3.1

Plan the writing. Draw the following graphic organizer on the board. You may also wish to distribute the matching graphic organizer located on page 120. Use the following think-alouds to model how to complete the graphic organizer. Ask for student input as you fill in the chart on the board.

- *The writing prompt asks me to form an opinion. How important do I think it is for everyone to recycle? After reading the passage, my opinion is that it is very important for everyone to recycle.*

- *Now I will think about the second part of the prompt. It asks me to find evidence from the passage to support my opinion.*

- *I will record my evidence—or reasons and supporting details—in the second part of each row on the chart. I will also show where I got my information.*

- *To finish my writing, I need a concluding statement or paragraph. I will restate my opinion by telling why I think it is very important for everyone to recycle.*

Reason 1: When we throw things into the trash, they go to a landfill. (paragraph 3)	**Supporting Details:** 1. Trash in landfills just stays there. 2. It pollutes the air and water. 3. Landfills aren't good for people or Earth.
Reason 2: We are sending too much trash to landfills. (paragraph 4)	**Supporting Details:** 1. Only some people recycle. 2. Landfills will be full soon. 3. We'll have to make more landfills.
Reason 3: Recycling helps people. (paragraph 5)	**Supporting Details:** 1. It creates jobs. 2. It saves money.

My Opinion Restated (Conclusion):

It is very important for everyone to recycle. This will help people and Earth.

Read and analyze the model. Distribute the student writing model and checklist on pages 10–11 to students. Read it aloud. Discuss with students whether or not the writer was successful at accomplishing the task. Ask them to complete the checklist as you discuss the opinion/argument piece.

Read the passage below.

Recycle It!

1. When something is recycled, it is reused in a different way. Recycled items are not thrown into the trash. They are sent to a recycling center instead. Workers there remove useful materials from each item. Then they use these materials to make new items. For example, pulp is a material in paper. Workers might use the pulp from old paper to make new paper.

2. Just about everything can be recycled. Paper, cardboard, and plastic can be recycled. Glass, metal, tin cans, and old clothing can be recycled too. Recycling is one important way to help Earth.

3. When we throw used items into the trash, they go to a landfill. A landfill is a large piece of land. The trash in landfills just stays there. It isn't reused in any way. Some trash contains chemicals. These chemicals can pollute our air and water. Landfills aren't good for people. They aren't good for our planet either.

4. Some people in our country recycle. But many more people need to do this. We are still sending too much trash to landfills. Many large truckloads of trash are dumped into landfills every day. Soon there won't be any more room in these landfills. Then we will have to make more landfills. We will have to cut down many trees to do this. This will cause animals to lose their homes. Some kinds of animals might become extinct. This means that they won't be around in the future. Recycling can help prevent this. It is the best way to reduce the amount of trash sent to landfills.

5. Recycling has other benefits too. It can create jobs. If people send more items to recycling centers, more workers will be needed there. It also saves money. For example, paper sent to recycling centers is often used to make new paper. This costs less than having to cut down trees to make new paper. Recycling makes our world a better place.

(continued)

(continued)

6. Recycling is always best. But you can also reduce waste by doing the following:

   • Bring cloth bags to the grocery store. Use these bags instead of plastic bags.

   • Drink water from reusable containers. Don't drink water from plastic bottles.

   • Write on both sides of a piece of paper.

   • Don't buy items in single-serving containers. For example, instead of buying juice boxes, buy a bottle of juice. The packaging used in single-serving containers is wasteful.

   • Whenever possible, buy products made from recycled materials.

Read and analyze the prompt.

Opinion/Argument Prompt

How important do you think it is for everyone to recycle? Use evidence from "Recycle It!" to support your opinion.

COMMON CORE
STATE STANDARD
W.3.1

Read and analyze the model.

Why Everyone Should Recycle

by Sarah Rinaldi

People in our country are throwing away too many things. It is very important for everyone to begin recycling right away.

Things that are not recycled are thrown into the trash. This trash goes to a landfill. Nothing is done with the trash in a landfill. It just sits there. It pollutes our air and water. Therefore landfills are bad for people and Earth.

Our landfills will be full soon too. Then we will have to make more landfills, which means we will have to cut down many trees. It is better to recycle because we can reduce the amount of trash being sent to landfills by recycling.

Recycling is also good in other ways. It creates jobs. If more and more people recycle, more jobs will be created at recycling centers. Recycling also saves money. For example, it costs less to make new paper from old paper because trees do not have to be cut down.

These are the reasons why I believe that everyone, and not just some people, should recycle. It is important because it will help keep people and our planet healthy.

✔ Writing Checklist: Opinion/Argument

- ❏ The writer introduced the topic.
- ❏ The writer stated a strong opinion, position, or point of view.
- ❏ The writer used well-organized reasons to support her opinion.
- ❏ The writer supported her reasons with facts and details from the text.
- ❏ The writer used linking words and phrases to connect her opinion and reasons, such as *because*, *therefore*, *since*, and *for example*.
- ❏ The writer ended with a conclusion that sums up and supports her position.
- ❏ The writer reviewed her writing for good grammar.
- ❏ The writer reviewed her writing for good capitalization, punctuation, and spelling.

COMMON CORE
STATE STANDARD
W.3.1

Writing an Opinion/ Argument

Mini-Lesson 2: **Writing to Multiple Texts**

COMMON CORE STATE STANDARD W.3.1

Write opinion pieces on topics or texts, supporting a point of view with reasons.

a. Introduce the topic or text they are writing about, state an opinion, and create an organizational structure that lists reasons.

b. Provide reasons that support the opinion.

c. Use linking words and phrases (e.g., *because, therefore, since, for example*) to connect opinion and reasons.

d. Provide a concluding statement or section.

Explain to students that they will often encounter writing prompts that instruct them to respond directly to more than one passage. For example, they might have to read two informational passages about the same topic or two fiction passages by the same author. Then take the following steps to guide students through the process of writing an opinion/argument in response to multiple texts.

Read the passages. Distribute pages 14–17 to students. Depending on students' needs, you may wish to read the passages aloud, have students read them with a partner, or have them read the passages independently.

Read and analyze the prompt. Read the prompt at the bottom of page 17 with students. Model how to analyze the prompt. Ask questions such as the following:

- *What form of writing does the prompt ask for?* (opinion/argument)

- *How can you tell?* (The prompt is asking what I think about the topic.)

- *What is the purpose of the assignment?* (state my opinion and support it)

- *What information do I need to complete the task?* (I need to use evidence from both "Guinea Pigs" and "The Best Pets for Apartment Living.")

COMMON CORE
STATE STANDARD
W.3.1

Plan the writing. Draw the following graphic organizer on the board. You may also wish to distribute the matching graphic organizer located on page 121. Use the following think-alouds to model how to complete the graphic organizer. Ask for student input as you fill in the chart on the board.

- *The writing prompt asks me to form an opinion. Do I think a guinea pig is a good pet to have if you live in an apartment? After reading both passages, my opinion is that a guinea pig is a great pet to have if you live in an apartment because guinea pigs are friendly, easy to tame, and spend a lot of time in a cage.*

- *Now I will think about the second part of the prompt. It asks me to find evidence from both "Guinea Pigs" and "The Best Pets for Apartment Living" to support my opinion.*

- *I will record my evidence, or reasons and supporting details, in the chart.*

- *To finish my writing, I need a concluding statement or paragraph. I will restate my opinion by telling why I think a guinea pig is a great pet to have if you live in an apartment.*

My Opinion:

I think a guinea pig is a great pet to have if you live in an apartment because guinea pigs are friendly, easy to tame, and can spend a lot of time in their cages.

Text 1:	Text 2:
"Guinea Pigs"	"The Best Pets for Apartment Living"
Supporting Evidence:	**Supporting Evidence:**
1. Guinea pigs are friendly and easy to tame.	1. Many small animals can live happily in a cage. A guinea pig is one of these animals.
Supporting Evidence:	**Supporting Evidence:**
2. They are quiet most of the time.	2. They can become very tame.

Read and analyze the model. Distribute the student writing model and checklist on pages 18–19 to students. Read it aloud. Discuss with students whether or not the writer was successful at accomplishing the task. Ask them to complete the checklist as you discuss the opinion/argument piece.

Read the passages.

Guinea Pigs

1. Guinea pigs are larger than hamsters but smaller than rabbits. They can have either short or long fur. They are friendly and easy to tame. A guinea pig makes a great pet.

2. If you keep a guinea pig as a pet, it will get to know you. When it does, it will squeak when you come into the room. This means that the guinea pig is happy to see you! Guinea pigs are very gentle and rarely bite.

3. When guinea pigs get excited, they jump straight up and down. This is called "popcorning." Guinea pigs are quiet most of the time. But they sometimes make purring and clucking sounds.

4. Guinea pigs are social animals. They enjoy being around people. In time, a guinea pig will trust its human companion. It will let a person pet it. Guinea pigs also like to be around other guinea pigs. If a person keeps two guinea pigs as pets, they usually become great friends. They will chase each other around and play.

5. A guinea pig is easier to take care of than a dog or cat. Guinea pigs do not mind staying in their cage most of the time, especially if it is large enough to run around in.

6. Since guinea pigs like to hide, they appreciate cardboard tubes and plastic coffee cans in their cages. They also like to climb, so they like rocks and bricks in their cages as well.

(continued)

(continued)

7. But even though a guinea pig might not visibly complain about being in its cage, it will like to spend some time out of its cage with its human companion. A guinea pig should be taken out of its cage at least four to five times a week for an hour or so each time.

8. Spending time with a guinea pig will give it a chance to know its human friend, so both human and animal will gain a lot from the experience.

(continue to next passage)

(continued)

The Best Pets for Apartment Living

1. Do you live in an apartment? If you do, you might not be allowed to keep a dog or a cat as a pet. Or you might feel that your apartment is just too small to share with a large, furry friend. Don't fret though. Many smaller creatures are well suited to apartment living and make great pets!

2. Don't rule out fish. You can't cuddle with fish or take them out of their tank to play. But they are beautiful and fun to watch. Fish are quiet, and they won't damage your apartment. Research shows that watching pet fish swim relaxes you.

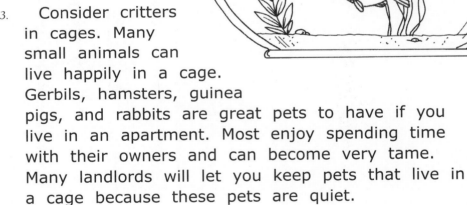

3. Consider critters in cages. Many small animals can live happily in a cage. Gerbils, hamsters, guinea pigs, and rabbits are great pets to have if you live in an apartment. Most enjoy spending time with their owners and can become very tame. Many landlords will let you keep pets that live in a cage because these pets are quiet.

(continued)

Common Core Writing to Texts Grade 3 • ©2014 Newmark Learning, LLC

(continued)

4. A feathered friend might be for you. A small bird can live happily in an apartment. Most are intelligent and can become tame enough to sit on your finger. Be sure to choose a smaller bird, such as a parakeet or a finch. Larger birds squawk loudly and may annoy your neighbors.

5. Don't forget about crabs. Hermit crabs are perfect apartment pets. A hermit crab lives in a shell, but this shell is not part of its body. If you put a few new shells in a hermit crab's tank, it might leave its old shell and move into a new one. Hermit crabs like to live with other hermit crabs, so you should keep a few together in a tank.

Read and analyze the prompt.

Opinion/Argument Prompt

Do you think a guinea pig is a good pet to have if you live in an apartment? Why or why not? If you do not think it would be a good pet, suggest one that you think would make a better choice. Use evidence from both "Guinea Pigs" and "The Best Pets for Apartment Living" to support your opinion.

COMMON CORE
STATE STANDARD

W.3.1

Read and analyze the model.

Why a Guinea Pig Is a Great Pet for an Apartment

by Michael Connelly

A guinea pig is a great pet to have if you live in an apartment because guinea pigs are easy to tame. A pet guinea pig also spends a lot of time in a cage.

Guinea pigs get to know their owners and are fun to watch. For example, your guinea pig might squeal when you come into the room because it is happy to see you. Once your guinea pig trusts you, it will let you take it out of its cage and will let you pet it. It is a good idea to take a guinea pig out of its cage at least four or five times a week for an hour or so each time. This gives you and your guinea pig a chance to become best friends.

Guinea pigs are quiet and do not mind spending most of their time in their cages. Because of this, many landlords will let you keep a guinea pig in your apartment.

Therefore because a guinea pig is friendly, tame, and quiet, and spends most of its time in a cage, I think it is a great pet to have if you live in an apartment.

✔ Writing Checklist: Opinion/Argument

❏ The writer introduced the topic.

❏ The writer stated a strong opinion, position, or point of view.

❏ The writer used well-organized reasons from both passages to support his opinion.

❏ The writer supported his reasons with facts and details from the texts.

❏ The writer used linking words and phrases to connect his opinion and reasons, such as *because*, *therefore*, *since*, and *for example*.

❏ The writer ended with a conclusion that sums up and supports his position.

❏ The writer used correct grammar.

❏ The writer used correct capitalization, punctuation, and spelling.

COMMON CORE
STATE STANDARD
W.3.2

Writing an Informative/ Explanatory Text

Mini-Lesson 3: Writing to One Text

COMMON CORE STATE STANDARD W.3.2

Write informative/explanatory texts to examine a topic and convey ideas and information clearly.

a. Introduce a topic and group related information together; include illustrations when useful to aiding comprehension.

b. Develop the topic with facts, definitions, and details.

c. Use linking words and phrases (e.g., *also, another, and, more, but*) to connect words within categories of information.

d. Provide a concluding statement or section.

Explain to students that they will often encounter informative/explanatory writing prompts that instruct them to respond directly to a passage they have read. Tell them that the passage might be an informational passage or fiction. Then take the following steps to guide students through the process of informative/explanatory writing in response to one text.

Read the passage. Distribute pages 22–23 to students. Depending on students' needs, you may wish to read the passage aloud, have students read it with a partner, or have them read it independently.

Read and analyze the prompt. Read the prompt at the bottom of page 23 with students. Model how to analyze the prompt. Ask questions such as the following:

- *What form of writing does the prompt ask for?* (informative/ explanatory)

- *How can you tell?* (The prompt is asking me to explain something and provide information.)

- *What is the purpose of the assignment?* (to explain a topic and give information about it)

- *What information do I need to complete the task?* (I need to use evidence from the passage "Interview with Dr. Sheila Fernandez, a Paleontologist.")

COMMON CORE
STATE STANDARD
W.3.2

Plan the writing. Draw the following graphic organizer on the board. You may also wish to distribute the matching graphic organizer located on page 122. Use the following think-alouds to model how to complete the graphic organizer. Ask for student input as you fill in the chart on the board.

- *The writing prompt asks me to explain what a paleontologist is and the kind of work he or she does.*

- *Now I will think about the second part of the prompt. It asks me to find evidence from the passage to support my explanation.*

- *I will record my evidence, or reasons and supporting details, in the chart.*

- *To finish my writing, I need a concluding statement or paragraph.*

Main Points	Details
Paleontologists study different kinds of fossils.	animals plants even rocks
Paleontologists travel.	look for fossils take them back to museum
They also work at a museum.	write articles study fossils teach people

Read and analyze the model. Distribute the student writing model and checklist on pages 24–25 to students. Read it aloud. Discuss with students whether or not the writer was successful at accomplishing this task. Ask them to complete the checklist as you discuss the informative/explanatory text.

Read the passage below.

Interview with Dr. Sheila Fernandez, a Paleontologist

1. **Question:** Dr. Fernandez, what exactly is a paleontologist (pay-lee-ahn-TAH-luh-jist)?

2. **Answer:** That's a great question. Most people think a paleontologist is a scientist who studies dinosaurs. A paleontologist is actually a scientist who tries to learn what life was like millions of years ago. Some paleontologists do study dinosaurs. But others study plants. Some even study rocks.

3. **Question:** What do you study?

4. **Answer:** I study the fossils of animals with backbones. I do study dinosaurs. But I also study other animals. I study crocodiles, lizards, snakes, birds, and larger animals, such as saber-toothed tigers.

5. **Question:** What is a fossil?

6. **Answer:** A fossil is whatever remains from an animal that lived long ago. A fossil might be a bone or a footprint. Over time, a bone or a footprint will turn to stone. Then it is a fossil.

7. **Question:** Where do you work, and what do you do at your job?

8. **Answer:** I work at a museum. My job requires me to do many different things. I travel a lot. I go to places where people have found fossils. I carefully remove these fossils from the ground. Then I take them back to the museum. This way, many people can study them. I write about these discoveries for newspapers and magazines.

(continued)

Common Core Writing to Texts Grade 3 • ©2014 Newmark Learning, LLC

(continued)

9. I also study the many fossils that are already at the museum. I try to figure out as much as I can about each animal from its fossil. I sometimes also teach at the museum. I tell people who come there what we have discovered.

10. **Question:** What's your favorite part of your job?

11. **Answer:** I like to travel to interesting places and meet new people. I don't mind getting dirty and spending my days digging. Every day is different. I really like that about my job.

12. **Question:** Is there anything you don't like about your job?

13. **Answer:** I don't like working outdoors in bad weather. When we're uncovering fossils, we have to work even if the weather is bad. It might be very hot or very cold. It might be pouring rain or snowing. We have to keep on working.

14. **Question:** What advice would you give to someone who wants to become a paleontologist?

15. **Answer:** Study hard in school. Try to do well in math and science. You have to go to college for many years to become a paleontologist, so it's important to be a good student. Try to be curious and use your imagination.

Read and analyze the prompt.

Informative/Explanatory Prompt

Explain what a paleontologist is and the kind of work he or she does. Support your explanation with evidence from "Interview with Dr. Sheila Fernandez, a Paleontologist."

COMMON CORE
STATE STANDARD
W.3.2

Read and analyze the model.

The Job of a Paleontologist

by Roberta Miller

A paleontologist is a scientist who studies fossils to try to learn what life was like millions of years ago. Fossils are the remains of plants and animals that have hardened over time. There are different kinds of paleontologists and not all of them study dinosaurs. Some study animals. Others study plants or rocks.

Part of a paleontologist's job is to travel to different places to dig up fossils. Then the paleontologist might bring them back to a museum. Many people study the fossils.

Other times, a paleontologist might work in a museum. He or she might write articles or teach others. The paleontologist might also study fossils that are already in the museum.

Paleontologists try to learn as much as they can about the past from the fossils they study.

✔ Writing Checklist: Informative/Explanatory

❏ The writer started with a clear topic statement.

❏ The writer grouped related information in paragraphs.

❏ The writer developed her topic with facts, definitions, concrete details, quotations, or other information and examples from the text.

❏ The writer linked ideas and information effectively using words and phrases.

❏ The writer used precise language and terminology to explain the topic.

❏ The writer wrote a conclusion related to the information she presented.

❏ The writer reviewed her writing for good grammar.

❏ The writer reviewed her writing for capitalization, punctuation, and spelling.

COMMON CORE
STATE STANDARD
W.3.2

Writing an Informative/ Explanatory Text

Mini-Lesson 4: Writing to Multiple Texts

> **COMMON CORE STATE STANDARD W.3.2**
>
> **Write informative/explanatory texts to examine a topic and convey ideas and information clearly.**
>
> a. Introduce a topic and group related information together; include illustrations when useful to aiding comprehension.
>
> b. Develop the topic with facts, definitions, and details.
>
> c. Use linking words and phrases (e.g., *also, another, and, more, but*) to connect words within categories of information.
>
> d. Provide a concluding statement or section.

Explain to students that they will often encounter writing prompts that instruct them to respond directly to more than one passage. For example, they might have to read two informational passages about the same topic or two fiction passages by the same author. Then take the following steps to guide students through the process of writing an informative/explanatory piece in response to multiple texts.

Read the passages. Distribute pages 28–31 to students. Depending on students' needs, you may wish to read the passages aloud, have students read them with a partner, or have them read the passages independently.

Read and analyze the prompt. Read the prompt at the bottom of page 31 with students. Model how to analyze the prompt. Ask questions such as the following:

- *What form of writing does the prompt ask for?* (informative/ explanatory)

- *How can you tell?* (The prompt is asking me to explain something and provide information.)

- *What is the purpose of the assignment?* (to explain a topic and give information about it)

- *What information do I need to complete the task?* (I need to use evidence from the passage "Life in Alaska" and the encyclopedia article about Alaska.)

Plan the writing. Draw the following graphic organizer on the board. You may also wish to distribute the matching graphic organizer located on page 123. Use the following think-alouds to model how to complete the graphic organizer. Ask for student input as you fill in the chart on the board.

- *The writing prompt asks me to explain how both passages support the idea that it is difficult to live in Alaska during the winter.*

- *Now I will think about the second part of the prompt. It asks me to find evidence from both passages to support my explanation.*

- *I will record my evidence, or reasons and supporting details, in the chart.*

- *To finish my writing, I need a concluding statement or paragraph.*

COMMON CORE
STATE STANDARD
W.3.2

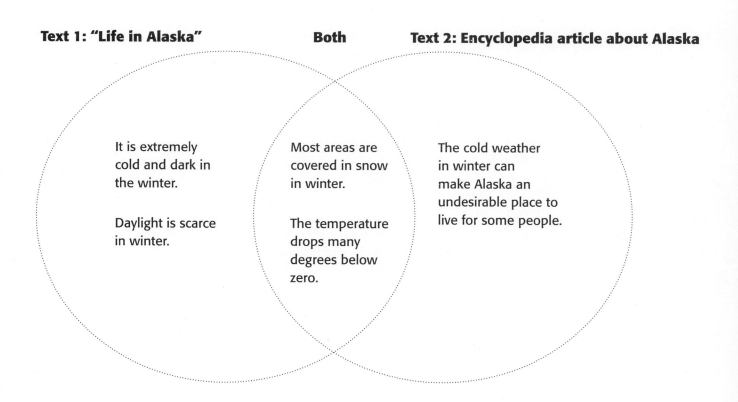

Text 1: "Life in Alaska" **Both** **Text 2: Encyclopedia article about Alaska**

It is extremely cold and dark in the winter.

Daylight is scarce in winter.

Most areas are covered in snow in winter.

The temperature drops many degrees below zero.

The cold weather in winter can make Alaska an undesirable place to live for some people.

Read and analyze the model. Distribute the student writing model and checklist on pages 32–33 to students. Read it aloud. Discuss with students whether or not the writer was successful at accomplishing this task. Ask them to complete the checklist as you discuss the informative/explanatory text.

COMMON CORE
STATE STANDARD
W.3.2

Read the passages.

Life in Alaska

1. When many people think of Alaska, they shiver. They imagine Alaska as a cold, dark place—and they are right. Alaska is extremely cold and dark during the winter. However, in the summer, the sky brightens, the temperature rises, and Alaska becomes incredibly beautiful.

Surviving the Difficult Winter

2. Most people who live in Alaska love it there. But even they complain about the cold during the winter. On the coldest days, the temperature drops many degrees below zero. And, of course, it snows often during the winter.

3. Most of Alaska is covered in deep snow throughout the winter. It is difficult to drive a car on snow-covered roads. Some people travel from place to place on sleds pulled by teams of dogs. In many places, lakes and rivers freeze and turn into thick ice during the winter. Children are able to ice skate on the frozen lakes.

4. Daylight is scarce during the winter. The sun rises late in the day and sets early. People spend most of the day in the dark. For example, in December in the city of Anchorage, the sun doesn't rise until about 10:00 A.M. and sets at about 3:30 P.M. This means that people have about five hours of daylight.

(continued)

(continued)

Enjoying the Beautiful Summer

5.   In the summer, Alaska becomes a beautiful place. The temperature is much warmer. The frozen rivers and lakes melt. People can now travel in boats and canoes. Flowers bloom throughout the wilderness, and animals seem to be everywhere.

6.   Because it is warmer, fish live in the rivers during the summer. Many people who live in Alaska like to fish during the summer. However, people need to be very careful when they go fishing in Alaska. Animals such as bears come out of hibernation during the summer. It isn't uncommon to see a giant moose in the nature areas outside of major cities.

7.   Children in Alaska enjoy long days of play during the summer. The sun rises very early in the summer and sets late at night. In Anchorage, the sun rises at about 4:30 A.M. and does not set until 11:30 P.M. People enjoy about nineteen hours of daylight!

(continue to next passage)

(continued)

Alaska—

1. Alaska is the largest state in the United States. It is twice the size of Texas, the second-largest state. Despite its large size, Alaska has one of the smallest populations of any state in the country. The cold weather in winter can make Alaska an undesirable place to live for some people. It is not uncommon for winters to be colder than -29°C (-20°F).

2. Alaska is known for its wilderness. The land is a mix of forests and glaciers, which are large walls of ice. The Yukon River in Alaska is one of the longest rivers in the world. Alaska's Mount McKinley is the highest mountain peak in the world.

3. Many people visit Alaska each year to catch a glimpse of animals they would not otherwise see. These animals include grizzly bears, moose, walruses, seals, and humpback whales, as well as many species of birds.

4. Alaska is well known for the Iditarod, its famous dogsled race. Most places in Alaska are covered in deep snow in the winter, so it is a perfect place for a dogsled race. The race is a celebration of Alaska's winter. Thousands of people gather each year in Anchorage, the capital of Alaska, to see the start of the race.

5. Sixty-two mushers, the men and women who guide the sleds, compete in the race. Each musher's sled is pulled by twelve to sixteen sled dogs. Mushers race more than 1,000 miles (1,609 kilometers) across mountains and frozen rivers and through thick forests. The race lasts from eleven to sixteen days.

(continued)

(continued)

Click the Links for
More Information About Alaska

 Businesses

 Cities

 Climate

 History

 Maps

 People

 Rivers

 Sights to See

 Weather

Wildlife

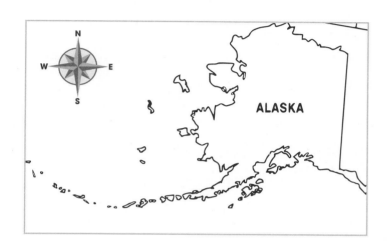

Read and analyze the prompt.

Informative/Explanatory Prompt

How do both passages support the idea that it is difficult to live in Alaska during the winter? Use evidence from "Life in Alaska" and the encyclopedia article about Alaska to support your response.

Read and analyze the model.

Alaska's Winter Weather

by Jeremy Fisher

It is difficult to live in Alaska during the winter because it is dark much of the time and extremely cold. Even people who live in Alaska and love it there complain that it is too cold in the winter. The temperature can drop many degrees below zero. There are only a few hours of daylight in the winter. Alaska is the largest state in our country, but not as many people live in Alaska as in other states. This is probably because people do not want to live in a place that gets so cold.

Another reason may be that it snows often in the winter in Alaska. Because of this, the ground in most places is covered with snow. Lakes and rivers freeze. Since it is difficult to drive a car on the roads, some people travel on a sled pulled by dogs. In fact, a famous dogsled race called the Iditarod is held in Alaska each winter. Sixty-two mushers guide sleds with twelve to sixteen dogs each for more than 1,000 miles.

While the summers in Alaska seem fairly typical, the winters are much colder and darker. Even though Alaska seems beautiful during the summer, the winters make it a difficult place to live.

✔ Writing Checklist: Informative/Explanatory

- ❏ The writer started with a clear topic statement.

- ❏ The writer grouped related information in paragraphs.

- ❏ The writer developed his topic with facts, definitions, concrete details, quotations, or other information and examples from both texts.

- ❏ The writer linked ideas and information effectively using words and phrases.

- ❏ The writer used precise language and terminology to explain the topic.

- ❏ The writer wrote a conclusion related to the information he presented.

- ❏ The writer reviewed his writing for good grammar.

- ❏ The writer reviewed his writing for capitalization, punctuation, and spelling.

Writing a Narrative

Mini-Lesson 5: Writing to One Text

COMMON CORE STATE STANDARD W.3.3

Write narratives to develop real or imagined experiences or events using effective technique, descriptive details, and clear event sequences.

a. Establish a situation and introduce a narrator and/or characters; organize an event sequence that unfolds naturally.

b. Use dialogue and descriptions of actions, thoughts, and feelings to develop experiences and events or show the response of characters to situations.

c. Use temporal words and phrases to signal event order.

d. Provide a sense of closure.

Explain to students that they will often encounter narrative writing prompts that instruct them to respond directly to a text they have read. The text may be fiction or informational. Then take the following steps to guide students through the process of writing a narrative piece in response to one text.

Read the passage. Distribute pages 36–37 to students. Depending on students' needs, you may wish to read the passage aloud, have students read it with a partner, or have them read it independently.

Read and analyze the prompt. Read the prompt at the bottom of page 37 with students. Model how to analyze the prompt. Ask questions such as the following:

- *What form of writing does the prompt ask for?* (narrative)
- *How can you tell?* (The prompt asks me to write a make-believe ending to a story.)
- *What is the purpose of the assignment?* (to write a new ending)
- *What information do I need to complete the task?* (I need to use evidence from the story "Trapped.")

COMMON CORE
STATE STANDARD
W.3.3

Plan the writing. Draw the following graphic organizer on the board. You may also wish to distribute the matching graphic organizer located on page 124. Use the following think-alouds to model how to complete the graphic organizer. Ask for student input as you fill in the chart on the board.

- *The writing prompt asks me to write a new ending to the story. I need to tell what the baby bird, the parent birds, and Grace and Lin do after the baby bird flies out of the storm drain.*

- *I need to make sure the events I include make sense based on the events in the story.*

- *I will record my events in the chart.*

- *To finish my writing, I need to include a new concluding statement for the story.*

Characters:	Setting:
Lin, Grace, Mr. Soto, birds, the neighbors	spring Lin's yard

Goal/Problem/Conflict:

The baby bird flies out of the storm drain.

Major Events:

1. Baby bird flies to the bush where its parents are.
2. The mother bird feeds it. The father looks on.
3. Lin and Grace see two other baby robins in the tree. They are happy to see that the baby bird is not hungry and is back with its family.
4. Mr. Soto and the neighbors slide the grate back over the storm drain.

Ending/Resolution:

Mr. Soto congratulates the girls on saving the baby bird.

Read and analyze the model. Distribute the student writing model and checklist on pages 38–39 to students. Read it aloud. Discuss with students whether or not the writer was successful at accomplishing the task. Ask them to complete the checklist as you discuss the narrative.

Read the passage below.

Trapped

1. Lin and Grace were enjoying the beautiful spring day. They had gone for a bike ride and were now playing hopscotch in Lin's driveway. As Lin bent down to pick up the stone she had thrown, she thought she heard a baby bird's cries. She glanced to her side and saw two full-grown robins frantically hovering over an area of the yard.

2. "I think a baby bird might be in trouble," she told Grace.

3. Grace looked over at the parent birds. "They look like they're really upset. Wait a minute—now I hear it, too. Maybe a baby bird fell out of its nest."

4. When the girls walked toward the robins, the bird flew into a nearby bush. Lin looked around the ground where they had been and saw a large storm drain. She peered down through the grate and saw a bird.

5. "Look!" she shouted. "A bird is trapped in there!" She tugged on the grate covering the drain, but it was incredibly heavy. "I'm going to get my dad."

6. Mr. Soto crouched down and looked at the bird. It opened its beak when it saw him and the girls laughed. "It thinks you're its mother," Lin said and giggled. "But isn't it too big to be a baby? It's almost as big as the other robins."

(continued)

(continued)

7. "It's a baby, but it's almost full-grown. It probably just left the nest. Somehow it must have fallen in there." Mr. Soto tried to slide the heavy grate, but it didn't budge. "The only way to get it out of here is to lift this grate, but it weighs a ton."

8. "I have an idea," Lin said. "What if Grace and I ask some neighbors to help? Do you think that would work?" Mr. Soto agreed that he could probably slide the grate off the drain if he had help.

9. Within a few minutes, the girls returned with several adults. They all grabbed hold of the grate. "On the count of three," Mr. Soto said. "One, two, three!" They pulled up hard and lifted the grate. Then they slid it to the side. Frightened, the little bird crouched down on the bottom of the storm drain. However, when it saw the open sky, it flapped its wings hard and flew out of the drain. Lin, Grace, Mr. Soto, and their neighbors cheered.

Read and analyze the prompt.

Narrative Prompt

Write a new story that tells what happens after the baby bird flies out of the storm drain. Tell what the baby bird, the parent birds, and Lin and Grace do. Your ending should make sense based on the events in the story.

COMMON CORE
STATE STANDARD
W.3.3

Read and analyze the model.

Trapped No More!

by Melissa Millano

Lin, Grace, and the adults watched the baby bird fly into the bush, where its parents were waiting. The baby bird opened its beak wide, and the mother bird put something inside it. "What do you think she fed it?" Lin asked.

"I don't know," replied Mr. Soto. "Maybe a berry from that bush."

"Look!" Grace shouted. "There are two other baby birds in the bush."

"That's great," Mr. Soto said. "Now the baby bird is back with its family."

Mr. Soto and the neighbors lifted the grate again and slid it back over the storm drain while Lin and Grace watched the birds. Afterward, they all thanked the neighbors again and said good-bye.

Mr. Soto turned to the girls. "You two should be very proud of yourselves. You did a really good thing today. You saved that little bird."

Lin smiled at Grace. "We sure did," she said.

Common Core Writing to Texts Grade 3 • ©2014 Newmark Learning, LLC

COMMON CORE
STATE STANDARD
W.3.3

✔ Writing Checklist: Narrative

- ❏ The writer established a setting or situation for her narrative.

- ❏ The writer introduced a narrator and/or characters.

- ❏ The writer organized her narrative into a sequence of unfolding events.

- ❏ The writer used dialogue and description to develop events and show how characters respond to them.

- ❏ The writer used time words to show the sequence of events.

- ❏ The writer used concrete words and phrases and sensory details to describe events.

- ❏ The writer wrote a conclusion to the events in her narrative.

- ❏ The writer reviewed her writing for good grammar.

- ❏ The writer reviewed her writing for capitalization, punctuation, and spelling.

Writing a Narrative

Mini-Lesson 6: Writing to Multiple Texts

> **COMMON CORE STATE STANDARD W.3.3**
> **Write narratives to develop real or imagined experiences or events using effective technique, descriptive details, and clear event sequences.**
> a. Establish a situation and introduce a narrator and/or characters; organize an event sequence that unfolds naturally.
> b. Use dialogue and descriptions of actions, thoughts, and feelings to develop experiences and events or show the response of characters to situations.
> c. Use temporal words and phrases to signal event order.
> d. Provide a sense of closure.

Explain to students that they will often encounter writing prompts that instruct them to respond directly to more than one passage. For example, they might have to read two fictional passages by the same author or two informational passages about the same topic. Then take the following steps to guide students through the process of writing a narrative piece in response to multiple texts.

Read the passages. Distribute pages 42–45 to students. Depending on students' needs, you may wish to read the passages aloud, have students read them with a partner, or have them read the passages independently.

Read and analyze the prompt. Read the prompt at the bottom of page 45 with students. Model how to analyze the prompt. Ask questions such as the following:

- *What form of writing does the prompt ask for?* (narrative)

- *How can you tell?* (The prompt asks me to write a letter from the point of view of a character.)

- *What is the purpose of the assignment?* (to write a letter, to compare Ben's behavior to Grasshopper's, and to explain how Ben can change his behavior)

- *What information do I need to complete the task?* (I need to use details from the story "Adam and Ben" and from the play "The Ant and the Grasshopper.")

COMMON CORE
STATE STANDARD
W.3.3

Plan the writing. Draw the following graphic organizer on the board. You may also wish to distribute the matching graphic organizer located on page 125. Use the following think-alouds to model how to complete the graphic organizer. Ask for student input as you fill in the chart on the board.

- *The writing prompt asks me to write a letter from Adam to Ben comparing Ben's behavior to Grasshopper's in "The Ant and the Grasshopper."*

- *Now I will think about the second part of the prompt. It asks me to explain what Ben should do to change his behavior in the future.*

- *I will list the points I will make in the letter in the graphic organizer.*

- *To finish my writing, I need a concluding statement or paragraph.*

Details from the Story
1. Like Grasshopper, Ben wanted to spend time playing instead of doing his work.
2. Like Grasshopper, Ben waited until it was almost too late and needed help from a friend.
New Details (in sequence)
1. Listen to your teacher.
2. Don't spend time playing when there is work to be done.
3. Spend time with Adam studying well in advance.
Conclusion
Ben would be happier if he didn't put off tasks until the last minute.

Read and analyze the model. Distribute the student writing model and checklist on pages 46–47 to students. Read it aloud. Discuss with students whether or not the writer was successful at accomplishing this task. Ask them to complete the checklist as you discuss the narrative piece.

Read the passages.

Adam and Ben

1. When Ms. Martin told her third-grade students that they had a book report due in two weeks, they groaned. Ashley quickly raised her hand. "Ms. Martin, we have too much work to do before the end of the year. It's only two weeks away! We're never going to get it all finished on time," she said.

2. Ms. Martin smiled. "Yes, you will—if you plan. Do some work every day and you'll be fine. Don't wait until the last minute to start studying and writing your book report. If you do, you'll get into trouble." Then the bell rang, and the students headed home.

3. "Wait up, Ben!" called Adam. Ben turned around and smiled. "Do you want to come to my house tonight and study? I can't believe we have so much work to do. We have tests, quizzes, and a book report. Maybe if we study and work together, it will be more fun," suggested Adam.

4. Ben shook his head. "Let's go the park instead. It's a beautiful day, and we have lots of time," Ben said.

5. "I think I'm going to study, Ben," replied Adam. "I'm going to listen to Ms. Martin and work every day so I don't get into trouble."

6. As the days passed, Adam found himself asking Ben the same questions again and again. "Do you want to go to the library after school? Do you want to talk about the book for the book report we have to do? How about we quiz each other on our spelling words?"

7. But Ben's answers were always the same. "It's a nice day. I want to play outside. We have plenty of time to do schoolwork."

(continued)

Common Core Writing to Texts Grade 3 • ©2014 Newmark Learning, LLC

(continued)

8.   As the end of the school year approached, Adam was proud of himself. He had spent a great deal of time studying for his tests and quizzes, and he had already written his book report. Ben, on the other hand, looked as if he had just seen a ghost.

9.   "What's wrong, Ben?" Adam asked.

10.   "Adam, I'm in big trouble. I didn't do any of my schoolwork yet."

11.   Adam raised his eyebrows. "That means you have to study for everything this weekend? Did you at least write your book report?" he asked.

12.   Ben shook his head and looked as if he might cry. "What am I going to do?"

13.   Adam sighed. "I'll help you study. I'll make flash cards and quiz you. Start by writing your book report tonight—and you'd better write it. Don't go outside. Stay in the house and do this," Adam scolded. "Then I'll come to your house tomorrow morning and help you study."

14.   Ben nodded. "Thanks, Adam."

15.   Ben and Adam worked all weekend. By Sunday night, Ben knew most of the material. He knew that he did not do his best, but he thought he might pass. After he had taken his last quiz and handed in his book report, he thanked Adam again.

(continue to next passage)

(continued)

The Ant and the Grasshopper
(an adaptation)

SCENE I

1. *It is a sunny summer day in a field.*

2. **NARRATOR:** Once upon a time, an ant and a grasshopper lived in a grassy meadow. The ant spent her days dragging large pieces of grain back to her home. She did this each day until she was too tired to work anymore. The grasshopper, on the other hand, spent his days singing and playing with his friends.

3. **GRASSHOPPER:** *(with another grasshopper and a butterfly)* Hi, Ant! Why do you work so hard, my friend? Why don't you come and play with us?

4. *(The second grasshopper and the butterfly dance and play.)*

5. **ANT:** It will soon be very cold. We will not have enough to eat when the ground is frozen. We must work hard now so that we are prepared for the future.

6. **GRASSHOPPER:** Nonsense! We should enjoy the beautiful weather while it is here. You're being silly. Let's play, my friends.

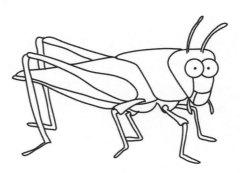

7. *(The three insects run off dancing and playing.)*

(continued)

(continued)

SCENE II

8. *(Everything is frozen, and a cold wind blows.)*

9. **NARRATOR:** Summer faded into autumn and autumn faded into winter. The days grew short and cold, and snow began to fall. The grasshopper didn't feel like singing and playing anymore. He was cold and hungry. He decided to ask Ant for help.

10. **GRASSHOPPER:** *(knocking on Ant's door)* I am cold and hungry, Ant. Please help me.

11. **ANT:** *(opens door)* All summer long I worked while you played. Now you have nothing to eat and you ask for my help. I will help you, my friend, but you must promise that next summer you will plan for the future.

12. **NARRATOR:** The grasshopper promised and thanked Ant for her help.

Read and analyze the prompt.

Narrative Prompt

Write a letter from Adam to Ben. In the letter, have Adam compare Ben's behavior to Grasshopper's in "The Ant and the Grasshopper." Have Adam explain what Ben should do to change his behavior in the future.

Read and analyze the model.

Adam's Letter to Ben

by Kyle Evans

Dear Ben,

We read "The Ant and the Grasshopper" in school today. I couldn't help but realize that you and Grasshopper acted the very same way. When Ant was busy gathering food for the winter, Grasshopper could not be bothered because he wanted to play in the warm weather. He thought he had plenty of time to do his work. When winter came, Grasshopper had to go to Ant and ask for help. He learned an important lesson: Don't wait until the last minute to prepare for the future.

You did the same thing as Grasshopper! You put off writing your book report and studying for your quizzes and tests until the last minute. You wanted to play outside instead of doing your work. Remember you said, "We have plenty of time to do schoolwork."

I helped you study or you might not have passed. You learned the same lesson that Grasshopper learned.

In the future, Ben, I think you should listen to your teacher. If she tells you to study a little bit every day, you should do this—even if it is a beautiful day. You should spend time studying with me early on. We both learn best by quizzing each other. If you do this, you'll do your best in school, and I want you to be happy.

Your friend,

Adam

✔ Writing Checklist: Narrative

❏ The writer established a setting or situation for his narrative.

❏ The writer introduced a narrator and/or characters.

❏ The writer organized his narrative into a sequence of unfolding events.

❏ The writer used dialogue and description to develop events and show how characters respond to them.

❏ The writer used time words to show his sequence of events.

❏ The writer used concrete words and phrases and sensory details to describe events.

❏ The writer wrote a conclusion to the events in his narrative.

❏ The writer reviewed his writing for good grammar.

❏ The writer reviewed his writing for capitalization, punctuation, and spelling.

Practice Texts with Prompts

How to Use Practice Texts with Prompts

This section of Writing to Texts provides opportunities for students to practice writing frequently in a wide range of genres and provides authentic practice for standardized writing assessments. Each practice lesson contains a passage or pair of passages followed by three prompts.

Before beginning, assign students one of the prompts, or ask them each to choose one. Explain to students that they are to plan and write an essay about the passage or passages according to the instructions in the chosen prompt. They should write on a separate piece of paper, or in a writing journal designated for writing practice.

There are various ways to use the practice section. You may wish to have students complete the writing tasks at independent workstations, as homework assignments, or as test practice in a timed environment.

If you choose to use these as practice for standardized tests, assign one prompt and give students 60 minutes to execute the task. In using these as test practice, tell students that they should think of their writing as a draft, and tell them they will not have additional time to revise their work.

You may also choose to have students respond to the prompts orally to strengthen academic oral language skills.

Graphic organizers for each type of writing are included on pages 120–125. You may choose to distribute them to help students plan and organize. On pages 126–127, reproducible Student Writing Checklists are provided. Distribute them to students to serve as checklists as they write, or as self-assessment guides.

Conducting Research

The Common Core State Standards require that students are provided opportunities to learn research techniques and to apply these skills in their preparation of projects. The passages in this section can make for research project starters. After students respond to an informational prompt, ask them to conduct further research on information from the practice text in order to build their knowledge.

Explain to students that researchers take good notes, connect new knowledge to what is already known, organize information into sensible layouts for a report, cite their sources, and use their own words to convey the information.

Tell students to gather information from print and digital sources. Have them take brief notes on sources and sort their facts, details, and evidence into categories. They may choose an appropriate organizer from pages 120–125.

Practice Texts with Prompts Table of Contents

COMMON CORE
STATE STANDARDS
W.3.1–
W.3.10

Name_____ Date_____

Read the passage below.

Spring Cleaning

1.   The sun rose high in the sky and warmed Earth. Birds were singing in the trees. Sophie woke up excitedly and ran to the window to look. "Spring is here at last!" she announced. "Finally I can go outside and play."

2.   It had been a very long, chilly winter. Sophie had been dreaming about all the fun things she would do outdoors when the weather improved.

3.   As Sophie raced toward the door, her parents stepped in front of her like a wall. "Wait one second, Sophie," said Mom. "You promised to help us clean the house once the weather improved."

4.   Sophie grumbled but remembered that she had promised to help with spring cleaning. "Okay, okay," she said, disappointed. "Where do we start?"

5.   All day, Sophie and her parents worked to clean the house. First she helped Mom clean the porch, where they found some of Sophie's favorite toys and sports gear. Then Sophie helped Dad scrub the doors and windows, which were dirty from dust and snow. That let the pretty sun shine brightly into the house.

6.   At last Sophie helped Mom take out their summer clothes and pack away their winter clothes. Sophie picked out her best T-shirt and shorts.

(continued)

Name_____ Date_____

(continued)

7. It was a long day of working, and Sophie was too tired to play outside at all. The next day, though, she awoke to find more beautiful weather waiting for her. She excitedly checked the window and then raced toward the door. Once again, her parents stepped in front of her to stop her. Sophie worried that she would have to work again today, too!

8. Instead, Dad handed her the T-shirt and shorts she had chosen. Mom gave her the baseball and basketball they had found on the porch.

9. "See?" said Dad. "Now the hard work is done and you can have fun!"

10. Sophie smiled and raced out the door, ready to enjoy the spring she had been waiting for.

COMMON CORE
STATE STANDARDS
**W.3.1–
W.3.10**

Name_____ Date_____

 Opinion/Argument Prompt

Do you think it is right for Sophie's parents to make her clean instead of going outside? Why or why not? Be sure to support your opinion with evidence and details from the story.

 Informative/Explanatory Prompt

Explain what Sophie is like as a person. Use details from the story to support your explanation. Use quotes from the story and summarize events that support your ideas.

 Narrative Prompt

Write a journal entry from Sophie's point of view telling what she did on the day she spent cleaning. Be sure to include her feelings about what she is doing. Use details from the passage to help you write your journal entry.

     Common Core Writing to Texts Grade 3 • ©2014 Newmark Learning, LLC

Name_____ Date_____

COMMON CORE
STATE STANDARDS
W.3.1–
W.3.10

Read the passage below.

The Wonderful Shirt

1. Nine-year-old Will Sully is looking at the clothes in his closet. He seems unhappy. His grandma is walking by in the hallway and stops to talk to him.

2. **Grandma:** You're getting so big and tall, Will! A lot of the clothes that fit you last year won't fit this year. Pick out whatever doesn't fit and we can give it to your little brother Jerry.

3. **Will:** But I don't want to give away my old clothes, Grandma. They're comfortable, and I'm used to them.

4. **Grandma:** Will, if they don't fit you anymore, what else can you do with them? They'll fit Jerry just right.

5. **Will:** Look, they still fit me. *(He tries putting on one of the old shirts. It is so small that it hardly fits over his head. He looks very silly. He and Grandma begin laughing.)* Okay, you're right. I'll give some of my clothes to Jerry.

6. **Grandma:** That's a good boy.

7. *(Will, looking grumpy, begins piling clothes on his bed. Then he takes out one bright red shirt.)*

8. **Will:** This is my favorite shirt ever! I can't give this away. It has to still fit me! (He tries to put on the shirt, but it is much too small. He sits sadly on the bed.) Oh no, it doesn't fit at all. Now I have to get rid of it.

9. *(Grandma returns with Jerry.)*

(continued)

COMMON CORE
STATE STANDARDS
W.3.1–
W.3.10

Name_____ Date_____

(continued)

10. **Grandma:** Jerry came to see what you're doing. He's excited to be getting some hand-me-downs from his big brother.

11. **Will:** Well, I'm not excited. I don't want to give up this great red shirt. Look, Grandma, it even has these letters written inside: "G.S." That means "Great Shirt."

12. **Grandma:** *(smiling)* Are you sure that's what it means?

13. **Will:** Well, no, I guess not, but it makes sense.

14. **Grandma:** Will, "G.S." means "George Sully." This shirt used to belong to your big brother George!

15. **Will:** But he's away at school.

16. **Grandma:** This was his shirt when he was younger.

17. He gave it to you when you were younger. Now it's your turn to be the big brother of the house.

18. **Will:** *(smiling)* I never thought of that. I guess I am biggest brother around here now!

19. *(Will gives a pile of shirts to Jerry. Then he writes "W.S." inside one nice blue shirt.)*

20. **Jerry:** Thanks, Will! But what does "W.S." mean?

21. **Will:** It stands for "Will Sully." But it can also stand for "Wonderful Shirt"!

Name_____ Date_____

Opinion/Argument Prompt

Is it a good idea to pass clothes down to younger family members? Why or why not? Support your opinion with evidence from the text and your own ideas.

Informative/Explanatory Prompt

Explain the lesson that Will learns in the play. Use details from the text to support your explanation.

Narrative Prompt

Write a thank-you letter from Jerry to Will. Use specific examples and details from the text in the letter. Use language that sounds like Jerry's voice, and include descriptions.

COMMON CORE
STATE STANDARDS
W.3.1–
W.3.10

Name_____ Date_____

Read the passage below.

Jack and His Friends
(An Adaptation of the Fairy Tale "Jack and His Comrades")

1. Long ago there was a boy named Jack. He lived with his mother in a nice little house, but he did not feel very happy. He wanted to make new friends and do important things. One day, Jack decided that he would go out into the world to make these wishes come true.

2. Jack wandered in the forests for days without any luck. Late one evening, though, he saw a donkey stuck in the mud. Jack carefully stepped out toward the donkey and helped it out of the mud. Grateful, the donkey promised its friendship to Jack.

3. As Jack and the donkey walked on, they found a lost cat. They made the cat feel comfortable and shared some food with it. The cat was pleased to join their little band of friends.

4. Shortly afterward, the group met a dog with a sliver in its paw. Jack removed the painful sliver, and the dog panted happily and joined their group.

5. Jack felt pleased that he had made some new friends, but he still had higher hopes. He wanted to do something truly important. He wanted to become a hero! It would be hard for a boy, a donkey, a cat, and a dog to become heroes. They would have to work together.

(continued)

Common Core Writing to Texts Grade 3 • ©2014 Newmark Learning, LLC

Name_____ Date_____

(continued)

6.   In a clearing in the woods, the group found a cabin. When they peeked through the window, they saw a robber counting his stolen treasures! Among the stolen goods were coins from Jack's neighbors and a necklace from his own mother!

7.   Jack knew he had to stop the robber. He and his new friends made a plan. They crept up close to the cabin. Then the dog began barking fiercely. This scared the robber, who ran outside to see what was happening. The sneaky little cat ran up to the robber and tripped him with its tail.

8.   Jack tied up the robber and placed all the stolen goods into a bag on the donkey's back. The strong donkey held the heavy bag easily. Now Jack and his new friends returned with the robber to the village as heroes. They returned the stolen goods and brought the robber to the police.

COMMON CORE
STATE STANDARDS
W.3.1–
W.3.10

Name_____ Date_____

 Opinion/Argument Prompt

Do you think Jack is a hero? Why or why not? Support your opinion with examples from the text.

 Informative/Explanatory Prompt

Write a summary of the story in your own words. Add a new title that highlights the most important idea from your summary.

 Narrative Prompt

Retell the story from the cat's point of view. Use dialogue and description in your story. Be sure to include details and characters from the original story.

Name_____ Date_____

COMMON CORE
STATE STANDARDS
W.3.1–
W.3.10

Read the passage below.

The Great Journey West

1.   Michael and Rachel Robinson were packing everything they owned into a covered wagon. They had decided to move to the West. They hoped to find some land and start their own farm. They imagined it would be a very exciting and beautiful trip.

2.   Michael and Rachel packed so many things that the wagon looked ready to break. Neighbors came out and warned them to be careful. "This trip may not be all fun and games," said one neighbor to Michael. Michael did not listen. He just smiled cheerfully and said, "Everything will be fine!"

3.   On April 5, 1848, Michael tied the wagon to an ox, and the strong animal began pulling it. Michael and Rachel began their great journey west.

4.   They traveled all day along a bumpy dirt trail to a meeting place in Missouri. They were surprised to see many other people with wagons hoping to move to the West. It was going to be a long, slow trip with so many other wagons on the trail.

5.   Shortly after they started, Michael saw the wagon wheels coming loose. The wagon was too heavy. They had to leave behind their heavy table and chairs. Then they had to get rid of their chest as well. That way there would be room to sleep inside the wagon when they got tired from walking.

(continued)

COMMON CORE
STATE STANDARDS
W.3.1–
W.3.10

Name_____ Date_____

(continued)

6. Along the way, Michael and Rachel became very hungry. Of all the things they had packed, they had not brought enough food! They had to trade some fancy silver plates for a bag of rice to eat. The trip was becoming much more difficult than they had expected!

7. After weeks of travel, Michael began to feel ill. Rachel took care of him, but they had to sell their nicest things to buy him medicine. Michael and Rachel then took the wrong path and got lost. That made their long trip even longer.

8. Just when they were almost too tired to continue, they finished their journey. They had made it to the West! Along the way they had to leave behind almost everything they owned. But they knew the important thing was that they had made it, and they still had each other.

Name_____ Date_____

COMMON CORE
STATE STANDARDS
W.3.1–
W.3.10

Opinion/Argument Prompt

Do you think Michael and Rachel are properly prepared for their trip west? Why or why not? Support your opinion with evidence from the text.

Informative/Explanatory Prompt

Summarize the problems Michael and Rachel have during their journey to the West. Be sure to include specific details from the text.

Narrative Prompt

Retell the story from Rachel's point of view. Include her thoughts and feelings about the journey. Be sure to include specific details from the text.

Name_____ Date_____

Read the passage below.

The Story of Medusa

1. Long ago in Greece there lived a terrible beast called Medusa. She had green skin and sharp teeth, and snakes instead of hair! The snakes had sharp teeth, too, and they would use them without pity. Medusa was so scary that anyone who dared to look at her turned into stone!

2. This awful monster lived in a cave outside town. The people of the town grew so afraid of Medusa that they would not leave their homes. Medusa did everything she could to scare them. Nobody could think of a way to stop her.

3. One day a young hero named Perseus arrived in town. He was surprised to see the people hiding indoors. When he heard about Medusa, he immediately decided to stop the terrible beast. Without wasting a moment, he began plotting his journey.

4. While Perseus prepared for his trip, two gods visited him. The first god, Hermes, gave Perseus special shoes with wings on them. The second god, Athena, gave Perseus a shield, a shiny metal plate that would help keep him safe. Perseus thanked the gods for their support.

5. The young hero walked toward Medusa's cave. He found that it was on top of a high mountain. It was too high to climb, so he used the winged shoes to fly up to it. Then he carefully walked into the cave. He called out, "Medusa, you have to stop spreading fear in the town!"

6. "Never!" shouted Medusa, jumping out of the shadows.

(continued)

Name_____ Date_____

(continued)

7.   Perseus remembered that he could not look at Medusa or else he would turn into stone. He also did not have a sword. How could he fight this monster? He knew she was too strong for him, so he would have to think of a clever plan to stop her.

8.   As Medusa ran toward him, Perseus looked at his shield. It was silver and so shiny that it looked like a mirror. He could see himself in it. This gave him an idea. He held up the shield to the monster.

9.   "Look at yourself, Medusa!" he said. Medusa saw her own face in the mirror-like shield. She turned into stone!

10.   Now the terrible beast was just a stone statue. The brave Perseus had saved all the people from the danger of Medusa.

COMMON CORE
STATE STANDARDS
W.3.1–
W.3.10

Name_____ Date_____

Opinion/Argument Prompt

Which character from the story do you think has the most unusual strengths and skills? Why? Support your opinion with events and details from the text.

Informative/Explanatory Prompt

Explain how Perseus defeats Medusa. Use details from the story in your explanatory text.

Narrative Prompt

Suppose Perseus took you with him to Medusa's cave, and you watched him defeat her. Write a story that describes the experience in your own words. Use details from the story.

Name_____ **Date**_____

Practice **6** Texts with Prompts

COMMON CORE
STATE STANDARDS
W.3.1–
W.3.10

Read the passage below.

Prairie Dogs

1. When does a "dog" look like a squirrel and live underground? When it is a prairie dog!

2. Prairie dogs are not the kind of dogs that people keep as pets. They are a kind of rodent, a group of animals that includes mice and squirrels.

3. These animals live in prairies, which are large, flat, grassy fields. Prairies stretch across a large area of North America.

4. Prairie dogs live in long tunnels, or burrows, that they dig underground. Many prairie dogs live together in "colonies." Some colonies get so large that people call them "towns." The largest prairie dog town was about the size of West Virginia.

5. Prairie dogs are about a foot tall and weigh almost four pounds. Their fur is fairly short and can be yellow, red, or brown.

6. Prairie dogs and pet dogs do have an interesting trait in common. They both bark! Prairie dogs make many kinds of barking sounds. Each sound has a different meaning. For example, a prairie dog may bark a certain way to warn others if danger is nearby.

Most prairie dogs live
in the shaded area.

(continued)

COMMON CORE
STATE STANDARDS
W.3.1–
W.3.10

Name_____ Date_____

(continued)

7.   In the cold of winter, when food is hard to find, prairie dogs may stay in their burrows all the time. In warm months, it is usually easy to see prairie dogs. Like many animals, they like to be outside during the day. They spend most mornings and afternoons looking for food.

8.   For a prairie dog, grass, leaves, and plant roots are a delicious treat. Sometimes prairie dogs eat farm crops or food for cows or horses. Many farmers become angry about this.

9.   Prairie dogs have a troubled history with farmers and ranchers. Beyond eating crops, they will also cut down vegetation to maintain a view of their area and they will eat the same grasses that would otherwise be available for cattle and horses.

10.   However, prairie dogs can also help the natural landscape. The prairie dog is an important part of the prairie ecosystem. Prairie dogs' digging brings air into the soil, which can allow for more water to go deeper into the soil. Their waste is also rich in a gas called nitrogen, which improves the quality of the soil and vegetation. The prairie dog also supports a wide variety of species in another way. Foxes, coyotes, weasels, snakes, hawks, eagles, and the endangered black-footed ferret are some of the many predators that rely on prairie dogs for food.

11.   If it looks like a squirrel and barks like a dog, it can be only one thing. It is a prairie dog!

Name_____ Date_____

COMMON CORE
STATE STANDARDS
W.3.1–
W.3.10

Opinion/Argument Prompt

If you were a farmer, would you want to live near a prairie dog town? Why or why not? Explain your point of view using facts and details from the text.

Informative/Explanatory Prompt

Explain how a prairie dog is similar to and different from the kind of dog people keep as pets. Use examples from the text to support your explanation.

Narrative Prompt

Imagine that you are a prairie dog. Write a story about a day in your life. Describe where you live, what you eat, and how you bark. Use details from the text to help you write your story.

Name_____ Date_____

Read the passage below.

Sequoyah: A Man of Many Words

1.   Imagine how hard it would be to write a letter or a story without the alphabet. The alphabet contains all the letters people need to make words. Without it, people would have no way of writing down their thoughts. A long time ago, the Cherokee people had a spoken language, but they had no written language. One man changed all that.

2.   Sequoyah belonged to the Cherokee, a group of Native Americans. He was born around 1776 and grew up to become a silversmith. A silversmith makes things from silver. He also married and had a daughter. In 1812, he and many other Cherokee became soldiers. They helped the United States fight in a war against Great Britain.

3.   At that time, Sequoyah started to think that his people needed an alphabet. The soldiers who spoke and wrote in English were able to write messages to loved ones back home. They could read letters and record information about events. The Cherokee soldiers could not do these things.

4.   After the war, Sequoyah returned home. He started working on a written language for his people. Over time, he came up with a set of eighty-five symbols. Each symbol was a letter-like shape. A few even looked just like letters from the English language. However, each symbol stood for a certain syllable in the Cherokee language. Syllables are groups of letters that make a certain sound. To sound out a big word, people say each syllable on its own.

5.   Sequoyah tested his new language by teaching it to his daughter, Ayoka. The language was simple, and she quickly learned how to read and write it. The new language was ready for use.

(continued)

Common Core Writing to Texts Grade 3 • ©2014 Newmark Learning, LLC

Name_____ Date_____

(continued)

6.   Sequoyah and Ayoka began showing others in their village how to use the language. In one case, Sequoyah sent Ayoka outside. Then he asked his cousin a question. His cousin answered, and Sequoyah wrote down what he said. When Ayoka came back inside, she read what Sequoyah had written. Sequoyah's cousin was shocked when Ayoka read his answer word for word.

7.   The new language spread quickly. In just a few months, thousands of Cherokee could read and write the new language. A few years after that, they published books, newspapers, and other materials. Sequoyah had forever changed life for the Cherokee.

COMMON CORE
STATE STANDARDS
W.3.1–
W.3.10

Name_____ Date_____

Opinion/Argument Prompt

At the end of the text, the author states, "Sequoyah had forever changed life for the Cherokee." Do you agree with this statement? Why or why not? Support your opinion with evidence from "Sequoyah: A Man of Many Words."

Informative/Explanatory Prompt

Why did Sequoyah want to invent a written language? Use details from "Sequoyah: A Man of Many Words" to support your explanation.

Narrative Prompt

Imagine what Sequoyah and Ayoka may have talked about before they showed their cousin how the language worked. Write a scene that uses dialogue and description to tell about this time. Use details from the text in your scene.

Name_____ Date_____

Read the passage below.

How to Make a Terrarium

1.   Looking at a beautiful garden on a cold, snowy day is sure to brighten anyone's mood. But there aren't many gardens blossoming in the middle of winter. When the weather is poor, enjoy the outdoors inside by making a terrarium, or bottle garden.

2.   Only a few items are needed to make a terrarium:

3.   • a clear glass container

4.   • plants

5.   • soil

6.   • rocks

7.   The first step in creating a terrarium is to choose the right plants. Choose plants that are alike and have the same needs. Some plants need warm, damp homes. Others grow better in places that are cool and dry. Select plants that will grow well together.

8.   Next, find a clear glass container to hold the plants. A large jar or bottle works well. The container must be big enough to hold all the plants and give them room to grow. Choose a container with a lid for plants that need warm, damp air. The lid will help hold in heat and water.

9.   After finding a container, cover the bottom with small rocks. The rocks will let water drain away from the soil. This helps keep the plants' roots from becoming too wet. Then top the rocks with soil. The soil should fill about half of the container.

(continued)

COMMON CORE
STATE STANDARDS

W.3.1–
W.3.10

Name_____ Date_____

(continued)

10. Now place the plants in the soil. Arrange them so they look nice, but remember to leave enough space for them to grow. Gently pat the soil down around each plant.

11. When finished planting, give the plants a drink. Remember to give the plants a little water every few days. Some plants, such as cactuses, need less water than this.

12. Finally find a place to keep the terrarium. Put it in a spot that gets a little sunshine every day. After that, it's time to enjoy this mini garden!

glass container

plants

soil

rocks

Name_____ Date_____

COMMON CORE
STATE STANDARDS
**W.3.1–
W.3.10**

Opinion/Argument Prompt

Do you think building a terrarium would be a good project for your science class? Explain to your teacher why or why not. Support your opinion with evidence from "How to Make a Terrarium."

Informative/Explanatory Prompt

Write a summary of the information in "How to Make a Terrarium" in your own words.

Narrative Prompt

Write a story about a character who is building a terrarium for a science fair. Use specific information from the text in your story. Make certain to use dialogue and description, and organize your writing in a series of events.

COMMON CORE
STATE STANDARDS
W.3.1–
W.3.10

Name_____ Date_____

Read the passage below.

The Real Story of Paul Revere

1. Many people know the story of Paul Revere. At least, they think they do. The legend of Paul Revere's ride to warn his fellow Americans that British soldiers were coming is famous. But it doesn't tell the story of what really happened on the night of April 18, 1775.

2. Great Britain ruled America at the time. Many Americans wanted to be free from British rule. The two sides argued about how the country should be run. People in America worried that this would lead to war.

3. Paul Revere was a silversmith in the city of Boston, Massachusetts. In 1775, he carried important messages and letters to American leaders. The legend says that one night Paul rode alone through the countryside, warning Americans that the British were preparing to attack. However this isn't completely true.

4. Paul was one of several riders sent to spread the word about the coming attack. His orders were to ride from Boston to the town of Lexington. One of the other riders was a man named William Dawes. He took the main road from Boston to Lexington. Paul rowed across the Charles River and then found a horse to take him to town. Along the way, he stopped to tell people the news.

5. In Lexington, Paul also warned two American leaders that British soldiers were coming to arrest them. After that, the legend says that Paul rode to Concord.

(continued)

Name_____ Date_____

(continued)

6. However this is not what actually happened. Paul met up with William Dawes and another rider named Samuel Prescott. The three men decided to ride on to Concord to warn the people there, but British soldiers stopped and arrested them.

7. William and Samuel escaped quickly, but Paul wasn't so lucky. The soldiers held him for some time, and he never made it to Concord. When the soldiers finally let him go, Paul returned to Lexington just in time to see the beginning of the battle that started the Revolutionary War. Paul fought in the war against the British.

8. The legend of Paul Revere grew over the years. During this time, the story of his famous ride hid some of the facts. But even though Paul was not a lone hero, he still played an important part in American history.

COMMON CORE
STATE STANDARDS
W.3.1–
W.3.10

Name_____ Date_____

 Opinion/Argument Prompt

Do you think Paul Revere was a hero? Why or why not? Support your opinion with evidence from the text.

 Informative/Explanatory Prompt

Explain what parts of the legend of Paul Revere are not true. Use details from the text to support your explanation.

 Narrative Prompt

Write a letter from Paul Revere to a friend discussing what happened on the night of April 18, 1775. Use descriptive details and write about the events in a sequential order.

Name_____ Date_____

Read the passage below.

Becoming a Writer
by Melanie Wallace

1.   I have always wanted to be a writer. As soon as I could speak, I started telling stories. Even before I learned to read and write, I made up all kinds of stories. I drove my parents crazy. I told imaginary tales about our neighbors. I invited imaginary friends to dinner.

2.   I once told a story by drawing pictures with markers. Unfortunately for my poor father, I did this on our dining room wall. He spent several hours trying to scrub off the marker but wound up having to repaint the room.

3.   Once I learned to read and write, I filled notebooks with stories, some real and some imagined. I once wrote a story about the day I met my baby brother Leo that made my mother cry. She said it was the sweetest thing she had ever read. Other times, I would imagine things—like what it might be like to live on the moon—and write a story about it.

4.   When I was in high school, I wrote for the school newspaper. I liked to write articles about special people. I wrote about a teacher who traveled all the way from Guam to teach in our high school in New Jersey.

5.   I entered one of my stories in a contest for young mystery writers. My story "The Case of the Missing Flounder" won second place. After this, a reporter from our town's newspaper wrote an article about me!

(continued)

COMMON CORE
STATE STANDARDS
W.3.1–
W.3.10

Name_____ Date_____

(continued)

6.   I kept writing while I was in college, but I became discouraged because so many of my short stories were rejected by magazines. My teachers told me that getting published sometimes takes years. But I felt bad that the editors of these magazines did not like my short stories.

7.   After college, I began writing a novel for young adults about life two hundred years into the future. The characters in my novel traveled from planet to planet and lived among aliens. Some of these aliens had special powers. One of them, Retro, was able to travel through time. Another, Jasmine, was able to move objects using only her mind.

8.   I submitted this book to a publisher. I was shocked when I received an acceptance letter. I was so happy. I felt that I had now reached my goal: I had become a writer.

Name_____ Date_____

COMMON CORE
STATE STANDARDS
W.3.1–
W.3.10

Opinion/Argument Prompt

Think about the text "Becoming a Writer." Would you like to read the author's novel? Why or why not? Support your opinion with details from the text.

Informative/Explanatory Prompt

What character traits describe the author when she was a child? Use details from the text to support your explanation.

Narrative Prompt

Write a journal entry from the author's point of view about the day she received the acceptance letter from the publisher about her novel.

COMMON CORE
STATE STANDARDS
W.3.1–
W.3.10

Name_____ Date_____

Read the passage below.

The Adventures of Helga

Chapter 4

1.   Helga searched her house for things she could use on her journey. She found a rope, some food, and a map. She placed these things carefully into her pack. Helga expected it would be a long trip. She would need all the help she could get.

2.   As she looked through her room, Helga felt an awful sadness. There was nothing on the corner of her bed. That was where Tom Cat, her cat and best friend, used to sit. Now Tom was lost somewhere, maybe very far away. Helga missed him so much that she could cry. At the same time, the idea made her feel stronger.

3.   "Tom, I promise I'll find you!" she called. "I won't rest until you're safe!"

4.   With that idea in her mind, Helga started her journey. She left the town and entered the woods. The trees were so leafy and thick that they blocked out the sun! The dark woods made Helga shake and shiver. She was brave, though, and kept going.

5.   A path led her to the edge of Shadow Swamp, a nasty, smelly place. There was green water on the ground. A group of frogs jumped past her. Helga smiled and laughed at the funny creatures. "Where are they going in such a hurry?" she wondered. "It looks like they are running away from something."

6.   Just then, Helga saw the two biggest snakes she had ever seen! She joined the frogs and tried to run away. The snakes were too fast though. They were about to catch her.

(continued)

Name_____ Date_____

(continued)

7.   Helga had to think fast. She began dancing, and the snakes followed her, trying to grab her feet. She danced faster and faster. By the time Helga had finished, the snakes had tied themselves in a knot!

8.   At last, Helga was safe from the snakes. She rested for a moment and then returned to her journey. She would not stop until she found Tom Cat.

Chapter 5

1.   After the scary events in the swamp, Helga hoped that the rest of her trip would be easier and safer. Right away, she saw this would not be the case. Ahead of her was Mighty Mountain. It was the tallest mountain in the land. Worse, it was owned by an ogre, a horrible beast.

2.   Helga had just begun to climb the mountain when she saw the ogre. She tried to sneak past him, but he spotted her. With a growl, he chased her into a cave! The cave was as dark as night. It was very hard to see. Luckily, Helga found a tiny crack in the rock. She was able to crawl out to safety. The big mean ogre was too large to squeeze through the crack. He was stuck in the cave, and again Helga was safe.

3.   The mountain was so high that it poked into the clouds. Helga could not see the top until she was almost there. When she reached the top, she saw a long bridge leading to another mountain far away. She began to walk toward the bridge when an elf stopped her.

(continued)

COMMON CORE
STATE STANDARDS
**W.3.1–
W.3.10**

Name_____ Date_____

(continued)

4. "Not so fast!" said the elf. "I'm not letting you cross until you prove how clever you are."

5. "And how would I do that?" asked Helga.

6. The elf asked her to answer a tricky question. His riddle went like this:

7.   "What reaches from here to there,
8.   Easily crisscrossing the air,
9.   Can only be crossed by those who dare,
10.   And it can lead you anywhere?"

11. "That's easy," said Helga. "It's a bridge!"

12. "That's right," said the elf. "Clearly you're a clever one. You may cross the bridge. Just don't look down!"

13. Helga said, "Thank you." She began crossing. She tried not to look down but could not help it. She peeked over the edge and saw how far away the ground was. Helga was so high up she began to feel a little scared.

14. When she reached the other side, she saw something in the mud. Footprints—cat footprints! She knew that Tom had gone this way! It was only a matter of time before she finally found him.

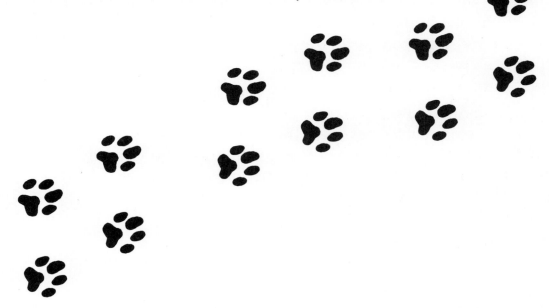

Name_____ Date_____

Common Core
State Standards
**W.3.1–
W.3.10**

Opinion/Argument Prompt

Think about the decisions Helga makes in both chapters. Choose a time when she has to make a decision. Tell what the decision is and whether or not you think she does the right thing. Explain your opinion using reasons from the text.

Informative/Explanatory Prompt

Explain why Helga is on a journey, and tell where she goes. Use details from both chapters of the book to support your explanation.

Narrative Prompt

At the end of Chapter 5, Helga sees cat footprints. Write a story to tell what happens next. Use details from Chapters 4 and 5 to help you write Chapter 6.

Name_____ Date_____

Read the passages.

Batter Up!

1. I grip the bat in both my hands
2. And hold my head up tall,
3. Cast a glance toward all the fans,
4. And tip my hat to all.

5. The cheering crowd grows louder
6. As they start to chant my name
7. And I couldn't be any prouder
8. To help my teammates win this game.

9. I dig my toe into the dirt,
10. Eye the pitcher on the mound,
11. Wipe some sweat upon my shirt,
12. And tap the bat upon the ground.

13. The pitcher winds up very fast
14. And hurls the ball my way.
15. As I swing, it whizzes past.
16. Strike one for me today.

17. The pitcher cracks a smile,
18. And then he lets another fly.
19. But this ball's just my style,
20. And I won't let it pass me by.

21. I swing with all my might.
22. The bat releases a loud *CRACK!*
23. And as that ball takes flight,
24. I know it's never coming back.

25. My fans erupt in cheers
26. And smiles spread across their faces
27. As the ball disappears
28. And I run around the bases.

(continue to next passage)

Name_____ Date_____

COMMON CORE
STATE STANDARDS
W.3.1–
W.3.10

(continued)

Ralph at Bat

1.   Ralph looked around the baseball field. He could hardly believe his team had made it to the championship game. If Ralph's team won today, it would be the best team in the whole league.

2.   Ralph joined his team on the field. All the players practiced throwing and catching the ball to warm up. Soon it was time for the game to start.

3.   Ralph tied his shoelaces tightly. He straightened his red hat and tucked his red shirt into his gray pants. Ralph's team took the field first. The other team quickly struck out. The teams traded places, and Ralph took a seat on the bench in the dugout.

4.   When it was his turn to bat, Ralph stepped up to the plate. Ralph knew he wasn't the best batter, but he was going to do his best. Ralph swung at the first pitch and missed. Strike one. Ralph let the second pitch go by. Strike two. Ralph swung at the third pitch and missed again. Strike three.

5.   Ralph stared at the ground as he returned to the dugout. He sat on the bench and pulled his hat low over his eyes. Ralph was sure his teammates were angry. How could he have struck out during such an important game?

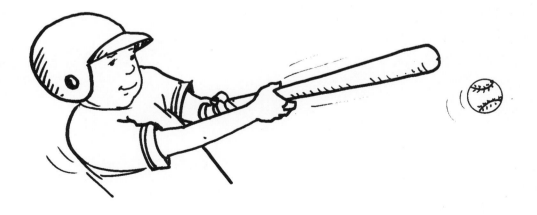

(continued)

Name_____ Date_____

(continued)

6. As the game continued, the score remained close. In the fifth inning, Ralph had another chance to bat. But he struck out again. With a red face, he returned to the dugout. Ralph couldn't even look at his teammates.

7. Finally the ninth inning came. The score was tied at six. The other team made three outs, and then Ralph's team was up. There were some base hits, putting a runner on third base and another on second. If the next batter could get a good hit and send a runner home, Ralph's team would win the game. But there were now two outs as well!

8. Suddenly Ralph felt very nervous. He was the next batter! What if he struck out again? He would let down his whole team.

9. Ralph's coach patted him on the back.

10. "You can do this, Ralph," he said. "Just keep your eye on the ball."

11. Ralph slowly walked to the plate. His hands shook a little. The pitcher threw the first ball. Ralph swung and missed. Strike one. The pitcher threw the second ball. Ralph watched it like a hawk. At the last second, he swung.

12. The bat hit the ball and sent it soaring into the outfield. Ralph raced to first base while the runner on third ran home. The game was over, and Ralph had helped score the winning run!

Name_____ Date_____

COMMON CORE
STATE STANDARDS
W.3.1–
W.3.10

Opinion/Argument Prompt

Think about the speaker of "Batter Up!" and the character Ralph. Which player do you think would make the best teammate? Support your opinion with reasons from both of the texts.

Informative/Explanatory Prompt

How are the speaker in "Batter Up!" and Ralph alike? Use specific examples from both the poem and the story to support your explanation.

Narrative Prompt

Write a narrative story from the point of view of the speaker in "Batter Up!" Imagine the speaker is a friend of Ralph's and their teams are playing in a championship game. Use details from both the poem and the story in your new narrative.

COMMON CORE
STATE STANDARDS
W.3.1–
W.3.10

Name_____ Date_____

Read the passages.

Why Man Has Fire
An Adaptation of a Myth from the Alabama Tribe

1. A long time ago, Bear owned Fire. Fire kept Bear and her family warm at night and helped them see in the dark. Fire cooked their food. Bear loved owning Fire and carried him everywhere.

2. One day, Bear and her family discovered many delicious acorns while walking through a forest. Bear had Fire in her arms. She carried Fire to the edge of the forest and set him down. Then she went back into the forest to feast on acorns with the rest of her family.

3. Fire had only a few pieces of wood left to burn. Without enough wood, he might go out. Fire was worried. "Bear!" he shouted. "I need you to feed me! I'm running out of wood to burn." But Bear was too far into the forest to hear him.

4. Just then Man walked through the forest and saw Fire. Fire had become very small. "Please feed me," Fire begged, "or I might burn out."

5. "What do you eat?" asked Man, who had never seen Fire before.

6. "Any kind of wood—I need to eat lots and lots of wood," explained Fire.

7. Man stepped into the forest and came out with several large sticks. He fed the sticks to Fire. Fire was still hungry, so Man fed him more and more sticks. Fire was so happy that he danced and roared in delight. Fire liked Man. Man promised to never let Fire feel hungry again.

8. When Bear finally came out of the forest, Fire yelled, "How could you do that to me? I almost burned out. I am going to stay with Man. He fed me plenty of wood."

9. Bear moved toward Fire to try to stop him from leaving with Man. Then Fire became angry and grew huge. He made so much heat that Bear and her family had to run away. And this is why Fire now belongs to Man.

(continue to next passage)

Common Core Writing to Texts Grade 3 • ©2014 Newmark Learning, LLC

Name_____ Date_____

COMMON CORE
STATE STANDARDS
W.3.1–
W.3.10

(continued)

How Fire Came to Hawaii
An Adaptation of a Hawaiian Myth

1. One day a long time ago, Maui's mother asked him to get her fish. Maui awakened his brothers, and they headed to the beach to go fishing. They put their canoe in the water and paddled far from shore.

2. When Maui looked back at the land, he saw a small fire on the side of a hill. "Fire!" he shouted and pointed to the hill.

3. At one time, people in Hawaii had fire to cook their food. They took hot coals from the great volcano Haleakala and brought them to their homes. But when the fire inside the volcano went out, they no longer had any fire. The people of Hawaii had to eat raw fish, fruit, and tree roots.

4. After they filled their canoe with fish, Maui and his brothers paddled back to shore. Maui quickly climbed the hill to see who had fire. He saw a group of birds called alae, or mud hens, scratching out the fire. Maui asked them to show him how to make fire, but they would not share their secret.

(continued)

COMMON CORE
STATE STANDARDS

W.3.1–
W.3.10

Name_____ Date_____

(continued)

5. The next week, Maui stayed behind when his brothers went fishing. He wanted to hide in the tall grass on the side of the hill so he could see how the alae made fire.

6. The alae are clever birds however. They counted the number of boys in the canoe and realized that Maui was not there. They decided not to make fire on that day.

7. But Maui was also clever. He rolled up some cloth in the shape of a person. The next time his brothers went fishing, he put the "person" in the canoe.

8. The alae counted the boys and believed that Maui was in the canoe when Maui was actually hiding in the tall grass watching them make fire!

9. Maui saw the birds gather pieces of dry wood and put them in a pile with some dry reeds. They rubbed two pieces of wood together until there were sparks. Then they lit the pile of wood on fire. Maui watched the birds cook their fish. It smelled delicious!

10. Maui ran home to share the secret of how to make fire with all the people in his village. People in Hawaii were able to cook food once again.

Name_____ Date_____

COMMON CORE
STATE STANDARDS
W.3.1–
W.3.10

Opinion/Argument Prompt

Think about the events in "Why Man Has Fire" and "How Fire Came to Hawaii." Do you think Bear and the alae birds are wronged by humans? Why or why not? Support your opinion with reasons from the text.

Informative/Explanatory Prompt

How are "Why Man Has Fire" and "How Fire Came to Hawaii" alike and different? Use specific examples from both texts to support your explanation.

Narrative Prompt

Imagine that Bear from "Why Man Has Fire" and the alae birds from "How Fire Came to Hawaii" met. Write a story about what they would do and what they would say about humans. Use details from both stories in your own original story.

COMMON CORE
STATE STANDARDS

W.3.1–
W.3.10

Name_____ Date_____

Read the passages.

The Messy Room

1.   "Mom!" Ian called. "Mack's here. We're going to the park to ride bikes. I'll be home before dinner."

2.   Ian's mother didn't reply but he heard her walking toward him. "This can't be good," he told Mack.

3.   "Ian, I told you that you can't go anywhere after school today until you clean your room—and you better do a good job."

4.   Ian rolled his eyes and looked at Mack. "This won't take long, maybe ten or fifteen minutes."

5.   "How about if I help you?" offered Mack. "It will get done faster that way."

6.   "Great. We'll be out of here in five minutes," Ian said.

7.   Ian opened the door to his room. Dirty clothes covered the floor and the bed. A laundry basket that may have contained clean clothes was now covered with dirty clothes. Shirts, shorts, jeans, socks, and shoes were everywhere.

8.   And dirty clothes weren't the only problem. Boxes, paper, pens, markers, and plastic bags were mixed into the mess. Glasses and dirty dishes were scattered about on Ian's dressers. His book bag, hockey stick, and skates were piled on his bed along with a basketball and, strangely, what looked like a bird's nest.

9.   Mack gasped. "There isn't even space to walk in here."

10.   Ian shoved aside some clothes on the floor, revealing the brown carpet underneath. "Sure there is! All we need to do is make some piles. Let's start by piling up the dirty clothes in the hallway."

(continued)

Name_____ Date_____

COMMON CORE
STATE STANDARDS
**W.3.1–
W.3.10**

(continued)

11. An hour later, Ian's arms were sore and the pile of clothes in the hallway was enormous. "I didn't even realize I had this much stuff," he said. Ian's mother appeared with several empty laundry baskets and offered to start hauling clothing to the laundry room.

12. Mack and Ian fetched several garbage bags from the kitchen. Mack held open a bag and Ian filled it with torn papers, old notebooks, broken pencils, and everything else he should have thrown away a long time ago. Mack picked up the bird's nest.

13. "Not that!" Ian shouted. "It fell out of the tree in the backyard. It must be from last spring. It's important to me." Mack laughed and placed the bird's nest on Ian's dresser.

14. Two hours later, all the dirty clothes were in the laundry room, the garbage was thrown out, and the dirty dishes were in the kitchen sink. Ian's things were placed neatly in the closet. The boys were ready to vacuum and dust.

15. "Do you still want to ride bikes?" Ian asked Mack.

16. "Nah, it's almost time for dinner. Let's just finish cleaning, and we'll ride bikes tomorrow after school. Just don't mess up your room!"

17. Ian laughed and thanked Mack for his help.

(continue to next passage)

COMMON CORE
STATE STANDARDS
W.3.1–
W.3.10

Name_____ Date_____

(continued)

Walking Chloe

1. When Aunt Emma told Ian that she was having trouble getting Chloe, her golden retriever puppy, to walk nicely on a leash, Ian offered to help. "Chloe and I are great friends," he said. "I think she'll listen to me."

2. The next day, Ian and his friend Mack stopped by Aunt Emma's apartment to take Chloe for a walk in the park. "Chloe's great and she loves me, so walking her is going to be easy," Ian promised Mack.

3. When Aunt Emma opened the door, Chloe jumped up on Ian and licked his face. Aunt Emma quickly snapped the leash onto Chloe's collar. She told Ian to hold onto the leash tightly and warned him that Chloe pulls hard sometimes. "It'll be fine," Ian assured her.

4. Mack, however, did not look so certain. "Chloe's so *big*," he said.

5. Ian calmly guided Chloe onto the elevator. As soon as the elevator doors opened, however, Chloe pulled on her leash so hard that Ian fell forward. Mack grabbed onto her leash and helped Ian back onto his feet.

6. They headed out of the building, with Chloe pulling all the way. Ian and Mack tried to calm her before going any farther. Finally she sat down. "That's a good girl," Ian told her. But then Chloe saw another dog, barked loudly, and bolted, dragging Ian for a bit before he made it to his feet. "I think this is going to be a little harder than I thought," Ian told Mack.

7. By the time the boys made it to the park and back, Ian had grass stains on his clothes and mud on his shoes and pants from the puddle Chloe had pulled him into. He and Mack both had blisters on their hands from trying to hold onto Chloe's leash.

8. Chloe collapsed on the floor of Aunt Emma's apartment. "Wow, look at that! She's actually tired," Aunt Emma said.

9. Ian plopped on the sofa. "Me, too!" he said.

Name_____ Date_____

COMMON CORE
STATE STANDARDS
W.3.1–
W.3.10

Opinion/Argument Prompt

Do you think Ian learns a lesson in both stories? Use specific details from both "The Messy Room" and "Walking Chloe" to support your opinion.

Informative/Explanatory Prompt

How would you explain the relationship between Ian and Mack? Give information about their relationship and about how they are alike and different. Use details and evidence from both stories to support your explanation.

Narrative Prompt

Write a story about something else that happens to Ian and Mack. Make sure your story has a beginning, middle, and end. Use details and other characters from both stories in your new story.

COMMON CORE
STATE STANDARDS
W.3.1–
W.3.10

Name_____ Date_____

Read the passages.

The Ant and the Dove
an adaptation of a fable by Aesop

1. Once upon a time, an ant was extremely thirsty. While he usually drank droplets of water from leaves or puddles, it hadn't rained in the forest in a very long time. The ant knew that he would have to travel to the river for a drink, but he was afraid to go so far alone. But the ant did not want to die of thirst, so he made his way to the river.

2. When the ant reached the river bank, he climbed down and drank the water. Before he knew it, he had slipped and fallen in. The fast current quickly carried him away. *I am going to drown for sure,* he thought.

3. A dove was sitting on a tree branch that was hanging over the water. She saw the ant and knew he was in terrible trouble. *If I don't do something, that poor little ant is going to drown*, she said to herself.

4. She quickly plucked a leaf from the tree and let it fall near the ant. "Grab onto the leaf!" she shouted.

5. The ant grabbed it and pulled himself up onto it.

6. Exhausted, he could barely move. He stretched out on the leaf and fell into a deep sleep. When he woke, the leaf had floated to the safety of the river bank. He climbed off the leaf and crawled up the river bank. "I am safe at last!" he yelled.

7. Then he saw a bird catcher holding a large net. She was sneaking up on the dove! "My friend is in big trouble," said the ant. The ant wanted to yell, but even if he screamed as loud as he could, the dove might not hear his tiny voice.

8. Then he had an idea. He crawled along the ground until he reached the bird catcher. He bit down hard on her foot. "Ouch!" she shouted. "I've been stung!"

9. The dove heard her cries and flew away quickly. The ant had saved the day.

(continue to next passage)

Name_____ Date_____

(continued)

The Serpent and the Eagle
an adaptation of a fable by Aesop

1. Once upon a time, an eagle sat perched high in a tree. She was hungry, so she was scanning the ground for her next meal.

2. Just then she saw a large serpent slithering on the forest floor. "That serpent will make a great meal," she said. "It's huge! Perhaps I will even share it with a friend."

3. The eagle flapped her large wings and flew high above the trees. Then she swooped down to the ground like a bolt of lightning. She grabbed the startled serpent in her large claws and flew into the air once again.

4. The eagle did not know that the serpent was strong and had a terrible temper. The serpent became very angry. "You will never eat me!" she shouted and wrapped her heavy body tightly around the eagle's legs. Then she squeezed hard.

5. The eagle cried out in pain. The pain in her legs and the weight of the serpent made it difficult to fly. She crashed to the ground, flapping her wings and rolling in the dirt, trying to free herself of the serpent, but it was no use. The serpent held on tightly.

6. The serpent was just about to bite the eagle and finish her off when she felt a pair of hands pull her off the eagle. She looked up to see a man toss her aside.

(continued)

COMMON CORE
STATE STANDARDS
W.3.1–
W.3.10

Name_____ Date_____

(continued)

7.   The eagle thanked the man and flew away. The man sat on a boulder to rest before continuing his journey through the forest.

8.   But the serpent grew angrier still. "How dare that man do that to me! He should be afraid of me. I am a poisonous snake, after all."

9.   She quietly slithered close to the boulder on which the man was resting and opened her mouth wide, revealing her sharp fangs.

10.   The man did not see the serpent, but the eagle did. She squeaked loudly and dove onto the serpent, this time hitting her hard and pushing her away from the man with her claws.

11.   Stunned, the serpent gave up and slithered deep into the forest. The man thanked the eagle for saving his life.

Name_____ Date_____

COMMON CORE
STATE STANDARDS
W.3.1–
W.3.10

Opinion/Argument Prompt

Which character in the fables do you think is the most clever? Support your opinion with details from both "The Ant and the Dove" and "The Serpent and the Eagle."

Informative/Explanatory Prompt

What lesson do the characters learn in both "The Ant and the Dove" and "The Serpent and the Eagle"? Use specific examples from the texts in your explanation.

Narrative Prompt

Imagine that the dove and the eagle were perched in the same tree. Write a scene in which they have a conversation about times when they had helped others. Use details from both fables in your story.

Common Core
State Standards
W.3.1–
W.3.10

Name_____ Date_____

Read the passages.

Why Our Town Needs Bike Racks

1. Dear Mayor Greenburg,

2. I think our town should have more bike racks. Adding more bike racks will encourage people to ride bikes into town for short trips. This would help our town in many ways.

3. If more people ride bikes, fewer cars will be on our roads. Cars give off harmful gases. These gases make the town's air dirty. Cars also create traffic. This makes it difficult for people to get where they need to go. People who are stuck in traffic make noise by beeping their horns.

4. Adding more bike racks will get cars off the road. It will also help make our town a cleaner and quieter place!

5. People should also ride bikes to get in shape and be healthy. Most people don't get enough exercise. We all need thirty minutes of exercise each day. Bike racks give people a safe place to store their bikes in town. People won't have to worry about their bikes while they do their errands.

6. Finally, adding more bike racks will save money. Our roads have more and more potholes every year. The weight from cars and trucks makes these holes. If more people ride bikes, there will be fewer cars on the roads. This means there will be fewer potholes. Our town won't have to spend money to fill in so many potholes.

7. For these reasons, I think our town should add more bike racks. It's a decision that will help everyone in our town!

8. Sincerely,

9. Amanda Lewis

(continue to next passage)

Name_____ Date_____

COMMON CORE
STATE STANDARDS
W.3.1–
W.3.10

(continued)

Why Our Town Shouldn't Add More Bike Racks

1. Dear Mayor Greenburg,

2.   I have heard that some people want our town to add more bike racks. Riding a bike is fun and a great way to stay in shape. And if more people ride bikes, there will be fewer cars on the road. This means that there will be fewer harmful gases in the air. However I don't think that adding more bike racks is going to make more people in our town ride bikes.

3.   Our town already has bike racks on Main Street and near the library. They are never filled with bikes. People don't drive cars because there aren't enough bike racks in our town. There are other reasons why they don't ride bikes.

4.   First the weather isn't always nice enough to ride a bike. It's much too cold to take a bike to town in the winter. And riding a bike in the snow is difficult, if not impossible. The roads in the summer are much better for bike riding. But even then, it isn't any fun to ride a bike if it's hot or rainy.

(continued)

COMMON CORE
STATE STANDARDS
W.3.1–
W.3.10

Name_____ Date_____

(continued)

5. The lack of cargo space on a bike is another reason why people drive in town. Many people go to town to buy groceries or other supplies. A bike doesn't have enough space to hold these items. An order of groceries won't even fit in a bike basket.

6. Bikes aren't practical for most families either. People with small children would have a hard time getting around town on bikes.

7. Lastly, adding more bike racks won't save the town money. The town must pay for the bike racks and then pay someone to put them up. We also have no way of knowing if the racks will ever be used. People may just decide to continue to drive their cars.

8. Adding more bike racks is a waste of money and will not make people want to ride bikes instead of driving cars.

9. Sincerely,

10. Michael Yang

Name_____ Date_____

COMMON CORE
STATE STANDARDS
W.3.1–
W.3.10

Opinion/Argument Prompt

Do you think bike racks encourage people to ride bikes instead of driving cars? State your opinion and use details from the letters to support your argument.

Informative/Explanatory Prompt

Use details from both letters to compare and contrast the arguments they make. What points do the letters have in common? How are the letters different?

Narrative Prompt

Imagine that you are Mayor Greenburg and that you have decided not to add more bike racks in town. Write a letter to the town newspaper explaining why you have made this decision. Be sure to address the points both Amanda and Michael made in their letters.

Name_____ Date_____

Read the passages.

Why Animals Migrate

1. When animals migrate, they move to a new place. Animals migrate for several reasons. They might need more food or water. They might need to be in a warmer climate to raise their young. While some animals migrate only a few miles, others travel great distances.

2. Most animals know by the changing seasons when it is time to migrate. To find their way, some animals use the sun and the stars as a guide. Others recognize familiar mountains, rivers, and lakes. Still others use their sense of smell or fly along the coastline.

3. Many types of birds migrate. These birds live in the North in the summer because the days are long and there is plenty of food. Then they head south to avoid the harsh northern winters.

4. Some birds stop to eat along the way during migration. Others eat a great deal before the trip. This extra food is stored as fat that their bodies can use for energy when they are traveling.

5. A bird called the bar-tailed godwit must do this. This little bird flies thousands of miles during migration. Because the godwit flies over water, it can't stop for a snack or a rest during its journey.

(continued)

Common Core Writing to Texts Grade 3 • ©2014 Newmark Learning, LLC

Name_____ Date_____

COMMON CORE
STATE STANDARDS
**W.3.1–
W.3.10**

(continued)

6.   Birds are not the only creatures that migrate. Many species of whales, such as the humpback and the baleen, also migrate. These whales live in northern waters in the summer because there is more food. Then they travel south to raise their young in warmer waters.

7.   Zebras in Africa migrate in a giant circle. They do this to follow the rainy seasons. When it rains in Africa, there is more food for zebras to eat.

8.   But the tiny ruby-throated hummingbird's migration may be the most amazing. These little birds are only three inches long and weigh about as much as a penny. Yet many travel from the North to the South and then cross the Gulf of Mexico. At a speed of about five miles per hour, the hummingbird flies across the large body of water without taking a break. This journey takes eighteen to twenty-four hours. Imagine running that fast for that long!

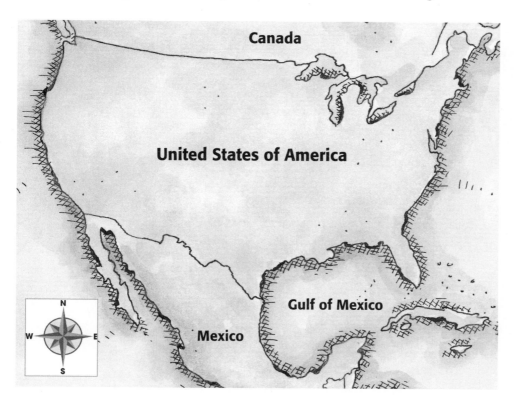

(continue to next passage)

COMMON CORE
STATE STANDARDS
W.3.1–
W.3.10

Name_____ Date_____

(continued)

The Amazing Monarch Butterfly

1. Beautiful orange-and-black monarch butterflies travel more than 2,000 miles (3,219 kilometers) each year. They do this because they can't survive the cold winter, and the nectar they eat becomes scarce. So they fly south—all the way from Canada and the northern United States to Southern California or Mexico, where the weather is warm.

2. Monarchs get ready to migrate as soon as the weather gets cooler, usually in October. They reach their winter home in Mexico in a few months. While in Mexico, monarchs cluster together in trees. Each butterfly uses its wings to cover the butterfly underneath it. This helps them stay warm. It also keeps them from blowing away.

3. During their trip back to the North, female monarchs lay eggs on the milkweed plants that grow along the way. These eggs hatch into tiny caterpillars that eat the leaves of the milkweed plants. A caterpillar will eat practically nonstop for weeks. Then it attaches itself to a leaf, sheds its skin, and forms a hard shell. About two weeks later, a full-grown monarch comes out of the shell. The butterfly then flies north.

4. Scientists still do not completely understand monarch butterflies' migration. Monarchs live only a few months, so each butterfly migrates only once. This means that each year, a new group of monarchs travels to Mexico. Yet the monarchs land in the exact same trees each year. How can the butterflies possibly know which trees to land in if they were never there before? Scientists also do not know how such small butterflies can find their way over such a long distance. They think the butterflies might use the sun like a compass. Scientists will keep studying monarchs until they solve the mysteries of their migration.

 Common Core Writing to Texts Grade 3 • ©2014 Newmark Learning, LLC

Name_____ Date_____

Opinion/Argument Prompt

The texts mention many animals and insects that migrate. Which creature's migration do you think is the most remarkable? Why? Support your opinion with reasons from both texts.

Informative/Explanatory Prompt

What are some reasons animals and insects migrate? Use information from both texts to support your explanation.

Narrative Prompt

Imagine that you are a monarch butterfly that meets a ruby-throated hummingbird on your migration south. Write a story about what happens and include what they might say to each other. Be sure to base your story on details from "Why Animals Migrate" and "The Amazing Monarch Butterfly."

COMMON CORE
STATE STANDARDS
W.3.1–
W.3.10

Name_____ Date_____

Read the passages.

Do Not Shorten Recess

1. Good evening,

2. My name is Janet Panero. I'm the mother of a third-grade student at High Town Elementary. I am here tonight to ask you to vote against shortening or eliminating recess at our school.

3. Some teachers, parents, and school board members think that recess should be shortened or eliminated entirely. They want children to spend more time in the classroom instead of playing outdoors. They think that recess is a waste of valuable time. They are wrong.

4. Recess is good for children. According to the American Academy of Pediatrics, unstructured play keeps kids healthy. It is not easy for an energetic child to sit at a desk for six or more hours a day. Children need to run and play. The students in our school have gym class only once a week. Recess is their only other chance to exercise. Research shows that students are better able to learn when they are allowed to exercise. They are less fidgety after they have had a chance to burn off some energy. Children who do not exercise have trouble concentrating. Therefore, more time in the classroom does not mean that our children will learn more. They can pay attention for only so long.

5. Recess also gives children a chance to socialize. Making friends is an important part of childhood. Most teachers do not allow students to socialize in class. Kids must sit quietly and work. At recess, children get to spend time together. They play together. Students learn social skills at recess. They learn how to get along with one another and to take turns.

6. My friends, please do not take this important time away from our students. Recess is only thirty minutes long. Shortening or eliminating recess is not a good idea. Let's do what's best for our children.

(continue to next passage)

Name_____ Date_____

(continued)

Recess Is Too Long

1. Ladies and Gentlemen,

2. As many of you know, my name is Kerry Walters. I am a third-grade teacher at High Town Elementary. I would like to take a few moments of your time to speak to you about why we need to shorten recess at our school.

3. Our children are allowed twenty minutes to eat lunch. They then go outside for thirty minutes of recess. For the first ten minutes of recess, our children play games and swing on swings. They exercise. This is obviously good for them.

4. But after this, many students become bored. This is when they get into trouble. The people who are in charge of recess struggle during this time. They break up quarrels. They have to deal with students who try to climb the fences surrounding the playground. They send students to the principal's office who try to climb on top of playground equipment instead of using it the right way. They spend this time disciplining kids. This is not fun.

(continued)

COMMON CORE
STATE STANDARDS
W.3.1–
W.3.10

Name_____ Date_____

(continued)

5.   Also, after about ten minutes of recess, some students want to get back inside the building. This is especially true when it is either very cold or hot outside. Students say that they are sick and need to see the nurse. They say that they need to see the principal. They ask to use the lavatory but then do not come back outside. These students are a burden on the people who work in the school's offices. It is not uncommon to see ten or more children just sitting in the school's offices waiting for recess to end.

6.   Lastly, when we asked students if they wanted a shorter recess, most of them said yes. They would rather have an extra fifteen or twenty minutes to work on homework or read a book. They would rather spend this time in the classroom.

7.   So please keep these points in mind when you vote this evening about whether we should shorten recess. Students who have too much unstructured time to play simply get into trouble.

Name_____ Date_____

COMMON CORE
STATE STANDARDS
W.3.1–
W.3.10

Opinion/Argument Prompt

Which speech do you agree with more? Why? Support your opinion with details from both speeches.

Informative/Explanatory Prompt

What do both speakers agree about? Support your explanation with specific examples from both speeches.

Narrative Prompt

Write a journal entry from the point of view of a student who does not want to go outside for recess. Use specific examples from both speeches.

COMMON CORE
STATE STANDARDS
W.3.1–
W.3.10

Name_____ Date_____

Read the passages.

Sherman School News

APRIL 28

Sherman School Holds Spelling Bee

1. The spelling bee has been making quite a buzz at Sherman Grade School!

2. On Thursday, April 25, Sherman School held its yearly spelling bee. The spelling bee is a contest in which children are given difficult words to spell. Children are out of the bee as soon as they misspell a word. The bee continues until there is just one student left, the winner.

3. More than one hundred people from the town came to watch. Some were parents and neighbors of the spellers. The crowd was excited. Members of the audience cheered.

4. The contest was an exciting one, for sure. Early on, Tania Leng looked like a winner. She spelled all her words correctly. She was calm and cool and made even the hard words seem easy! Tania's father was in the crowd clapping for her.

5. But the spelling bee had a surprise ending. Tania was close to winning but finally misspelled a word. She lost that last round to fellow Sherman speller Jake Ellis. Jake became Sherman's spelling bee champ!

6. After the contest, the spellers shook hands and clapped for one another. Jake received a prize for his good work. The children's teacher went on the stage to discuss how much work the children had done. The people in the crowd clapped again. Everyone seemed to be in a good mood.

7. "It was a wonderful evening," said Sherman teacher Klarissa Culp. "I'm so proud of our students," Mrs. Culp added. "They did so well tonight! I heard some great spelling, and everyone tried his or her best. That's the most important part of any contest."

8. The next spelling bee will be held in April of next year.

(continue to next passage)

Name_____ Date_____

(continued)

My First Spelling Bee
(Tania Leng's Journal)

Thursday, April 25

1.   I was just at my first spelling bee and it was great fun!

2.   I arrived at school at nine o'clock in the morning. People were setting up tables and chairs. I was going to sit on the stage in front of everyone! I found my seat and sat down. Someone gave me a paper that listed everyone in the spelling bee. I was excited to see my name, Tania Leng, on the list! But I also saw that many other clever boys and girls were in the bee as well. I hoped to do well but did not imagine I would win.

3.   As I sat there, I tried to stay calm and remember my practice. I had spent weeks learning new words. I learned the meaning and spelling of each word. Soon I had learned hundreds of words. Some were easy and some were very hard. Remembering all the hard work I did helped me stay calm.

4.   At 10 o'clock, the contest began! I felt excited and a little scared. I had to forget this nervous feeling so I could think about the words. I spelled them all correctly. My third word, "sandwich," was tricky. I almost spelled it "s-a-n-d-w-h-i-c-h" but luckily I remembered the right spelling.

5.   I was amazed that I was still in the bee after a whole hour. People clapped for me. I saw my father clapping the hardest of all. I could not believe it!

(continued)

COMMON CORE
STATE STANDARDS
W.3.1–
W.3.10

Name_____ Date_____

(continued)

6. Later in the competition, the words were even harder. I had to spell "February," "disappoint," and "kangaroo." Those are some tricky words! I kept trying to remember my practice. It also helped to picture the letters in my mind.

7. Soon there were only two students left standing. By this time I felt like I was going to win for sure. I stopped trying my hardest. When I got my word, I misspelled it! The word was "category" but I spelled "c-a-t-a-g-o-r-y." Everyone in the room became quiet. I knew I had gotten it wrong!

8. My mistake meant that another player, Jake Ellis, had a chance to win. He spelled his word, "knowledge," correctly and won.

9. I was sorry I didn't win, but I was glad I did so well. When people began clapping for Jake, I clapped too. Later I told him he did a great job, but next year I was going to try even harder!

Name_____ Date_____

COMMON CORE
STATE STANDARDS
**W.3.1–
W.3.10**

Opinion/Argument Prompt

Is the spelling bee a good subject for an article in the school newspaper? Why or why not? Clearly state your opinion and support it with details from both "Sherman School Holds Spelling Bee" and "My First Spelling Bee."

Informative/Explanatory Prompt

What can you tell about Tania Leng from both the newspaper article and her journal entry? Use details from the texts to support your explanation.

Narrative Prompt

Write a letter from Tania Leng to Jake Ellis congratulating him on winning the spelling bee. Use details from both "Sherman School Holds Spelling Bee" and "My First Spelling Bee" in your letter.

COMMON CORE
STATE STANDARDS
W.3.1–
W.3.10

Name_____ Date_____

Read the passages.

Ancient Egypt

1. The ancient Egyptians lived about 5,000 years ago. They lived in the deserts near the Nile River, the longest river in the world. Life for the ancient Egyptians centered on the river. Each spring, the river flooded. The flood made the soil near the river very rich and fertile. The ancient Egyptians were able to grow crops easily in this soil.

2. The Nile River also helped people in other ways. It gave them fresh water to drink and bathe in. They also used the river to travel from place to place by boat.

3. Work and family were very important to the ancient Egyptians. Most people were farmers, soldiers, artists, or scribes. Scribes were people who wrote documents for others. Most sons worked in the same job as their father. For example, if a father was an artist, his sons most likely became an artist. A son started training for his career when he was only about nine years old.

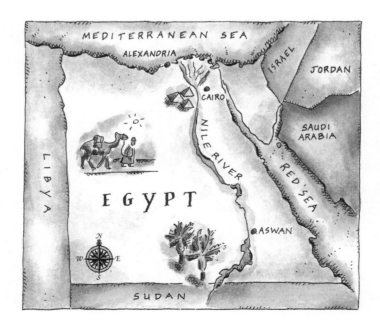

(continued)

Name_____ Date_____

(continued)

4. Mothers usually trained their daughters to run the household—and this was no easy task. It wasn't uncommon for ancient Egyptian families to have ten or more children, and all of them would live in the same house. Caring for so many people was a great deal of work. Women rarely had time to work outside of the home.

5. The ancient Egyptians built very large homes out of sun-dried bricks. Some homes had as many as thirty rooms. Each room had a special purpose. Homes in ancient Egypt had bedrooms, family rooms, bathrooms, and storage rooms.

6. Homes had flat roofs. People liked to sit on the roofs of their homes at night to enjoy a cool breeze.

7. When the ancient Egyptians were not working, they enjoyed spending time with family and friends. They held dinner parties with music. They spent time swimming and sailing.

8. Children were taught to respect their parents and older family members. They were expected to be kind and helpful. When they finished their chores, children played with board games and toys. People also played sports. They liked to race chariots, wrestle, and fish.

9. Most ancient Egyptian households had at least one cat. Cats helped people by keeping mice away from the grain they stored in their homes. But people back then believed that cats had a more important job than this. They thought cats had magical powers and would protect their homes from danger.

(continue to next passage)

Common Core
State Standards
W.3.1–
W.3.10

Name_____ Date_____

(continued)

Ancient Sumerians

1. The ancient Sumerians were the first civilization. Unlike the people before them, they did not travel from place to place in search of food. Instead they lived in one place and grew their own food. The ancient Sumerians lived about 6,000 years ago in Sumer, an area between two large rivers: the Tigris and the Euphrates. This area is now the country of Iraq.

2. It didn't rain often in Sumer. This made it difficult to grow crops. However the Sumerians dug canals from the rivers to their fields. They were able to bring water to their crops using these canals. They even used math and invented the first written language. This language was called cuneiform (kyoo-NEE-ih-form).

3. Many men in ancient Sumer were farmers and merchants, or people who bought and sold goods. Women were not considered equal to men, but they had more rights than women in other ancient societies. For example, women could buy and sell goods. Some women learned to read and write.

4. People in ancient Sumer lived in three-story houses built of mud bricks. These houses had a courtyard in the center and flat roofs. People cooked and slept on their roofs at night when the weather was very warm. Children were expected to obey their parents and older family members.

5. Only boys in ancient Sumer went to school. They learned to read and write in school. They also learned about the law and medicine. They copied their lessons onto clay tablets and studied them. Their teachers were very strict. Some of these boys became scribes, people who spent time writing. Others became teachers. Even though girls did not go to school, they could work outside the home if they wanted to. They could become weavers or cloth spinners. They could even start their own businesses.

Name_____ Date_____

COMMON CORE
STATE STANDARDS
W.3.1–
W.3.10

Opinion/Argument Prompt

Do you think your school's social studies program should include the ancient Egyptians and the ancient Sumerians? Support your opinion with reasons from both texts.

Informative/Explanatory Prompt

What was life like for girls in ancient Egypt and ancient Sumer? Use details from both texts to support your explanation.

Narrative Prompt

Imagine that you are a time traveler. Write a story that tells of your travels to 6,000 years ago to ancient Sumer, then 5,000 years ago to ancient Egypt. Use details from both texts in your story.

COMMON CORE
STATE STANDARD

W.3.1

W.3.4

W.3.5

Name_____ Date_____

Opinion/Argument Organizer

Reason 1:

Supporting Details:

Reason 2:

Supporting Details:

Reason 3:

Supporting Details:

My Opinion Restated (Conclusion):

COMMON CORE
STATE STANDARD
W.3.1
W.3.4
W.3.5

Name_____ Date_____

Opinion/Argument Organizer

My Opinion:

Text 1:

Text 2:

Supporting Evidence:

Supporting Evidence:

Supporting Evidence:

Supporting Evidence:

Common Core
State Standard

W.3.2

W.3.4

W.3.5

Name_____ Date_____

Informative/Explanatory Organizer

Main Points	Details

Name_____ Date_____

COMMON CORE
STATE STANDARD

W.3.2

W.3.4

W.3.5

Informative/Explanatory Organizer

Text 1:   **Both**   **Text 2:**

_____   _____

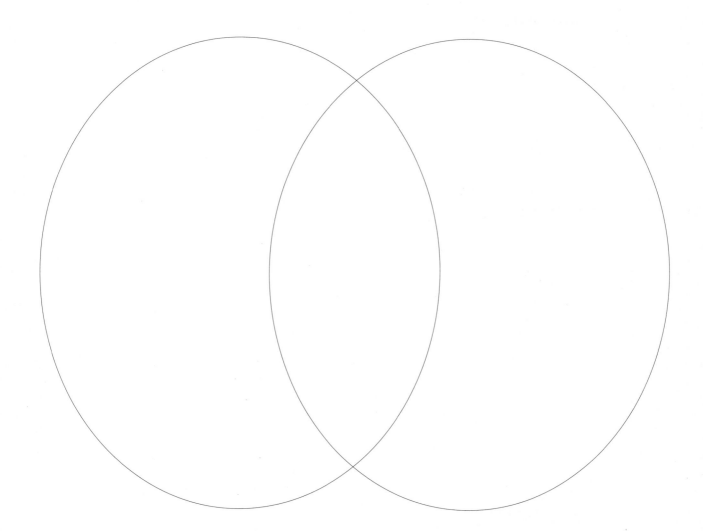

COMMON CORE
STATE STANDARD

W.3.3

W.3.4

W.3.5

Name_____ Date_____

Narrative Organizer

Characters:

Setting:

Goal/Problem/Conflict:

Major Events:

1.

2.

3.

4.

Ending/Resolution:

Name_____ Date_____

COMMON CORE
STATE STANDARD
W.3.3
W.3.4
W.3.5

Narrative Organizer

Details from _____

1.

2.

3.

New Details (in sequence)

1.

2.

3.

Conclusion

Common Core
State Standard

**W.3.1–
W.3.5**

Name_____ Date_____

✔ Writing Checklist: Opinion/Argument

- ❏ I introduced the topic.
- ❏ I stated a strong opinion, position, or point of view.
- ❏ I used well-organized reasons to support my opinion.
- ❏ I supported my reasons with facts and details from the text.
- ❏ I used linking words and phrases to connect my opinion and reasons, such as *because*, *therefore*, *since*, and *for example*.
- ❏ I ended with a conclusion that sums up and supports my position.
- ❏ I reviewed my writing for good grammar.
- ❏ I reviewed my writing for good capitalization, punctuation, and spelling.

✔ Writing Checklist: Informative/Explanatory

- ❏ I started with a clear topic statement.
- ❏ I grouped related information in paragraphs.
- ❏ I developed my topic with facts, definitions, concrete details, quotations, or other information and examples from the text.
- ❏ I linked ideas and information effectively using words and phrases.
- ❏ I used precise language and terminology to explain the topic.
- ❏ I wrote a conclusion related to the information I presented.
- ❏ I reviewed my writing for good grammar.
- ❏ I reviewed my writing for capitalization, punctuation, and spelling.

Common Core Writing to Texts Grade 3 • ©2014 Newmark Learning, LLC

Name_____ Date_____

✔ Writing Checklist: Narrative

❏   I established a setting or situation for my narrative.

❏   I introduced a narrator and/or characters.

❏   I organized my narrative into a sequence of unfolding events.

❏   I used dialogue and description to develop events and show how characters respond to them.

❏   I used time words to show my sequence of events.

❏   I used concrete words and phrases and sensory details to describe events.

❏   I wrote a conclusion to the events in my narrative.

❏   I reviewed my writing for good grammar.

❏   I reviewed my writing for capitalization, punctuation, and spelling.

Rubrics and Assessment

Using the Rubrics to Assess Students and Differentiate Instruction

Use the Evaluation Rubrics on the next page to guide your assessment of students' responses. The rubrics are based on the Common Core State Standards for writing. Similar rubrics will be used by evaluators to score new standardized assessments.

After scoring students' writing, refer to the differentiated rubrics on pages 130–135. These are designed to help you differentiate your interactions and instruction to match students' needs. For each score a student receives in the Evaluation Rubrics, responsive prompts are provided to support writers. These gradual-release prompts scaffold writers toward mastery of each writing type.

• For a score of 1, use the Goal-Oriented prompts.

• For a score of 2, use the Directive and Corrective Feedback prompts.

• For a score of 3, use the Self-Monitoring and Reflection prompts.

• For a score of 4, use the Validating and Confirming prompts.

Using Technology

If you choose to have students use computers to write and revise their work, consider these ways to support online collaboration and digital publishing:

• Google Drive facilitates collaboration and allows teachers and peers to provide real-time feedback on writing pieces.

• Wikis enable students to share their writing around a common topic.

• Audio tools enable students to record their works (podcasts) for others to hear on a safe sharing platform.

• Student writing can be enriched with images, audio, and video.

Evaluation Rubrics

Student _____ Grade _____

Teacher _____ Date _____

Opinion/Argument				
Traits	**1**	**2**	**3**	**4**
The writer states a strong opinion, position, or point of view.				
The writer supplies well-organized reasons that support his or her opinion using facts, concrete examples, and supporting evidence from the text.				
The writer links opinions and reasons using words and phrases.				
The writer provides a concluding statement or section.				
The writer demonstrates command of grade-appropriate conventions of standard English.				

Informative/Explanatory				
Traits	**1**	**2**	**3**	**4**
The writer introduces his or her topic with a main idea statement.				
The writer uses facts, definitions, and details to develop his or her points.				
The writer groups related information together.				
The writer uses linking words and phrases to connect ideas within categories of information.				
The writer provides a concluding statement or section.				
The writer demonstrates command of grade-appropriate conventions of standard English.				

Narrative				
Traits	**1**	**2**	**3**	**4**
The writer recounts a well-elaborated event or short sequence of events.				
The writer includes dialogue and descriptions of actions, thoughts, and feelings.				
The writer uses temporal words and phrases to signal event order.				
The writer provides a sense of closure to the narrative.				
The writer demonstrates command of grade-appropriate conventions of standard English.				

Key
1–Beginning
2–Developing
3–Accomplished
4–Exemplary

Comments

Opinion/Argument

TRAITS	1: Goal-Oriented
The writer states a strong opinion, position, or point of view.	When I start an opinion piece, I state my opinion or point of view. I need to tell exactly what my view is. After reading this prompt, I can state my position as ____.
The writer supplies well-organized reasons that support his or her opinion using facts, concrete examples, and supporting evidence from the text.	I need to think of two or three good reasons to support my opinion. My opinion about this prompt is ____. I'll jot down the evidence I need to support my opinion. Then I'll go back to my writing and include them.
The writer links opinions and reasons using words and phrases.	I need to link my reasons together using words and phrases, such as *because, therefore, since* and *for example*. I am going to look for places where I can add these words and phrases.
The writer provides a concluding statement or section.	When I finish writing an opinion piece, I need to finish with a strong statement that supports my whole argument. When I conclude this opinion piece, I can restate my position as ____.
The writer demonstrates command of grade-appropriate conventions of standard English.	I am going to read through my writing to make sure that I formed and used both regular and irregular verbs correctly. I will read through my whole opinion piece to make sure that I have spelled words correctly.

Common Core Writing to Texts Grade 3 • ©2014 Newmark Learning, LLC

2: Directive and Corrective Feedback	3: Self-Monitoring and Reflection	4: Validating and Confirming
Reread the first sentences of your writing. Then go back and reread the prompt. Did you clearly state an opinion that answers the prompt? Revise your statement to make it clear and focused.	Tell me how you chose _____ as your opinion. How can you make your position clearer for the reader?	I can see that your position is _____. You made your opinion very clear. That got me to pay attention to the issue.
What are your reasons for your opinion? Find supporting details and evidence in the text for each reason. Group these ideas together in separate paragraphs.	How did you decide to organize your ideas? Did you identify the information that was most important to include? How did you do this?	You included some strong evidence to support your opinion.
Let's read this paragraph. I see a reason and some evidence. How can you link these ideas together? I notice that you have more than one reason to support your opinion. What words can you add to show the reader that you are moving from one reason to another?	Show me a part of your opinion piece where you link ideas using words and phrases. Show me a part where you could improve your writing by using linking words or phrases.	The words and phrases _____ and _____ are very effective at linking together the connection between your opinions and reasons. They help me understand your ideas.
Reread the last sentences of your opinion piece. Does it end by restating your point of view? Go back and look at your opinion statement. How can you reinforce this idea in your conclusion?	How does your conclusion support your opinion or the position that you have taken? Is there a way you could make this conclusion stronger?	Your concluding section clearly supports our point of view. You've really convinced me that your point of view makes sense.
Read that sentence again. Does it sound right to you? Your noun and verb don't agree. How should you edit that? When you write a title, what do you need to do?	Show me a place in your writing where you used compound and/or complex sentences. Show me a place where you used commas correctly. What rule of punctuation did you apply?	Your opinion piece included many compound sentences and you remembered where the commas should go. I noticed you spelled many difficult words correctly.

Informative/Explanatory

TRAITS	1: Goal-Oriented
The writer introduces his or her topic with a main idea statement.	When I start an informational/explanatory text, I introduce my topic. I'm going to think about what I want my readers to know about ____. Then I create a main idea statement.
The writer uses facts, definitions, and details to develop his or her points.	I need to find facts and details from the text to support my points. I can go back to the text and underline parts that I think will help my writing. Then I will include them in my informative/explanatory text.
The writer groups related information together.	It is important that I group ideas together in an order that makes sense. I am going to categorize my information to help me structure the parts of my informative/explanatory text.
The writer uses linking words and phrases to connect ideas within categories of information.	I need to connect my ideas together using linking words, such as *also, another, and, more,* and *but*. I am going to look for places where I can add these words and phrases.
The writer provides a concluding statement or section.	When I finish writing an informative/explanatory text, I need to summarize my ideas in a conclusion. When I conclude, I can look back at my main idea statement, then restate it as ____.
The writer demonstrates command of grade-appropriate conventions of standard English.	I am going to read through my writing to make sure that I capitalized the beginning of each sentence, as well as the proper nouns I've used. I will make sure I have used quotation marks correctly when I've quoted directly from the text.

2: Directive and Corrective Feedback	3: Self-Monitoring and Reflection	4: Validating and Confirming
How could you introduce your topic in a way that tells exactly what you will be writing about?	Take a look at your main idea statement. Do you feel that it clearly introduces your topic?	Your main idea statement is clearly ____. That introduction helped me understand exactly what I was going to read about.
What are your main points? Find supporting details and evidence in the text for each point.	Have you included all of the facts you wanted to share about ____.	You included some strong facts, definitions, and details to support your topic.
Put your facts and details into categories. These categories can be the sections of your informative/explanatory text.	How did you decide to organize your ideas? Did you look at an organizing chart? How did it help you?	You organized your informative/explanatory text into [number] well-defined sections.
Let's read this paragraph. I see two related ideas. How can you link these ideas together?	Show me a part of your informative/explanatory text where you could improve your writing by using linking words or phrases.	The words and phrases ____ and ____ are very effective at linking together ideas.
Reread the last sentences of your informative/explanatory text. Do they restate your main idea?	Show me your concluding statement. Is there a way you could make this conclusion stronger?	After I read your conclusion, I felt I had really learned something from your writing.
Read that sentence again. Does it sound right to you? Your noun and verb don't agree. How should you edit that? Look at the word ____ in that sentence. Check your spelling.	Show me a place where you correctly used an irregular noun or verb. Where have you used an apostrophe correctly?	Your informative/explanatory text included many complex sentences. I notice you were very careful to check your spelling.

Narrative

TRAITS	1: Goal-Oriented
The writer recounts a well-elaborated event or short sequence of events.	I will use a sequence-of-events chart to jot down the events I will write about. I will record details from the text I have already read. I will include those details in my new narrative.
The writer includes dialogue and descriptions of actions, thoughts, and feelings.	I want to include descriptions in my narrative. I will write down words that will help my readers picture what I am writing about. Then I will include these in my narrative.
The writer uses temporal words and phrases to signal event order.	When I write a narrative, I need to use signal words so that my reader does not get confused. I will add words and phrases such as *first, then, the next day,* and *later that week* to help my reader understand the order of events.
The writer provides a sense of closure to the narrative.	I am going to reread the ending of my narrative to make sure that it gives the reader a feeling of closure. I need to concentrate on how the problem in the narrative is solved.
The writer demonstrates command of grade-appropriate conventions of standard English.	I am going to read through my narrative to make sure that I formed and used both regular and irregular verbs correctly. I am going to scan through my narrative to make sure I used end punctuation on every sentence.

2: Directive and Corrective Feedback	3: Self-Monitoring and Reflection	4: Validating and Confirming
Think of events that will lead from the problem to the resolution. You've decided to write about ____. Now think of the sequence of events you will include.	What graphic organizer could help you organize your narrative events? Tell me how you went about organizing your narrative.	The events you organized lead to a [fun, surprising, etc.] resolution.
Imagine that you're a character. What's happening in the narrative? What do you have to say to other characters? What do you have to say about the events?	Show me how you gave information about your characters and setting.	I can visualize where your narrative takes place. You've included some nice descriptive details.
Let's read this paragraph. Is it clear to the reader when all the action is taking place? What words could you add to help the reader's understanding?	Show me where you used sequence signal words in your narrative. Show me a place where you could use signal words to make the order of events clearer.	The phrase ____ gave a nice transition between ____ and ____.
Let's read the ending of your narrative. Does it show how the problem is solved? Is there something you can add to make sure the reader feels as if the narrative piece is over?	Show me how your ending gives the reader a feeling of closure. Are there any questions from the narrative that you feel were unanswered?	You've developed an interesting resolution to the problem in your narrative. It gives me a sense of closure.
I got confused about the sequence when ____. Take another look at your verb tenses. Make sure they are consistent. When you write a title, what do you need to do?	Show me a place in your writing where your sentences could be better. What could you do to improve them? Show me a sentence in which you changed the punctuation. How did you know it was wrong?	Your narrative included a lot of dialogue, and you used punctuation correctly. I notice you spelled many difficult words correctly!

Editing/Proofreading Symbols

Mark	What It Means	How to Use It
ℰ⁄	Delete. Take something out here.	We went to t̶o̶ the store.
∧	Change or insert letter or word.	San Franc̸ico, Cala̸fornia ∧is my home.
#	Add a space here.	My family∧loves to watch baseball.
◯	Remove space.	We saw the sail ͜boat streak by.
ℰ⁄	Delete and close the space.	I gave the man my mon̶n̶ey.
⌐⌐	Begin a new paragraph here.	"How are you?" I asked. ∧"Great," said Jack.
∽	No new paragraph. Keep sentences together.	The other team arrived at one. ⌐ The game started at once.
∾	Transpose (switch) the letters or words.	Thi͡er friends came with gifts.
≡	Make this a capital letter.	m̳r̳s̳. s̳mith
⁄	Make this a lowercase letter.	My S̸ister went to the C̸ity.
◯	Spell it out.	Mr. García has ③ cats.
⊙	Insert a period.	We ran home∧There was no time to spare⊙
∧	Insert a comma.	We flew to Washington∧D.C.
∨	Insert an apostrophe.	Matt∨s hat looks just like John∨s.
⟨⟨ ⟩⟩	Insert quotation marks.	⟨⟨Hurry!⟩ said Brett.
?	Is this correct? Check it.	The Civil War ended in 1875. ?
STET	Ignore the edits. Leave as is.	Her hair was∧brown. STET